The CARPE DIEM Way

5 Powerful Steps To Working From Anywhere
For Business Owners & Entrepreneurs

Author: Andy Willis

Adviser: Jaqui Lane

Designer: Arthur Luke

Proofreader: Clare Wadsworth

First published in 2021 by Working From Anywhere Pty Ltd

© 2021 Andy Willis

The moral rights of the author have been asserted

ISBN 978-0-6486929-6-6

Every effort has been made to trace and acknowledge the original source of material used within this book. Where the attempt has been unsuccessful, the publisher would be pleased to hear from the author/publisher to rectify any omission.

All rights reserved. Apart from any fair dealing for the purposes of private study, research, criticism or review, as permitted under the Australian Copyright Act 1968 and subsequent amendments, no part may be reproduced, stored in a retrieval system or transmitted by any means or process without written permission in writing from Andy Willis, andy@wfa.life

Printed and bound by IngramSpark

The ultimate guide to making **TIME** for **LIFE**.
Transition your business to operate from anywhere, at anytime, on any device

To Mum and Dad

For your brave decision to pack up to seek a better life for your children. Arriving into Australia in 1970 with five kids, two suitcases, no family support, no job and only £100 to your name.

For blessing me with your entrepreneurial spirit.

I thank you from the bottom of my heart.

Eternally Grateful

| About the author

Andy Willis is an entrepreneur, mentor and founder of Working From Anywhere.

Andy well knows the consequences of business taking over life. His successful Conference & Event Management business took him all over the world, yet he fell into the trap of deferring 'life' until 'later'.

Today he runs his WFA business from his beachside home in Australia, a village in the French Alps or on road trips in his customised WFA van with Belle, the Jack Russell by his side and time to ride a wave or cycle every day.

His Anywhere, Anytime, Any Device program sets business owners free, fulfilling his personal mission to help people start living The Carpe Diem Way.

| A book that will get your life back on track

"Seize the Day

I did this.

No, really, I did, way before I met Andy.

With my husband we seized every day of 22 years, travelling the world on boats. We are a little smug that we did our crazy stuff when we were young and fit.

BUT I wasn't running a company at the time. And this is where I wipe that smug smile off my face. We finished travelling and I started a business and I allowed it to consume me.

I dropped our ethos of 'live every moment as if it was our last'. There was so much to do, I had to be everything to everyone, I had to make it work. And to do all this I had to work 18 hours a day.

A year ago my physical and mental health suffered a great deal and despite easing that stress I am still paying for that, and paying for it dearly. At the time of the stressful period, I had not yet met Andy, but thank goodness I did shortly after. If I hadn't adopted the strategies in this book, I may not

be sitting here writing this. My Doctor said if I didn't change my life, I wouldn't have a life to change. Andy showed me how to do it.

Not only will this book help you steer your life back on track, but it will also rein it in so you, yourself are back at the helm and in control. Your life may just depend on it! You must take stress seriously.

This information is relatable and powerful. It is written in basic language, not bogged down with jargon. The straightforward step-by-step process will change your thinking and give you those AHA moments we all love.

As entrepreneurs, we must invest in time and set up at the beginning, or during growth. We must invest in our health and we must absolutely Seize the Day."

Jackie Parry, *Best selling author, entrepreneur, founder of SisterShip Training Pty Ltd, world traveller*

| Contents

Introduction   11
Why I wrote this book?   13
Who is this book for?   15
How this book works   17

Section 1:
Why the Carpe Diem Way?   21
The Conventional Way   27

Section 2.
The Mindset Shift: 46
Step 1 - The Foundation   64
Step 2 - Anywhere, anytime, any device   83
Step 3 - Getting the processes out of your head   125
Step 4 - Day to day operations from anywhere   151
Step 5 - Make TIME for LIFE   170

Section 3
The Time is Now - Start living life The Carpe Diem Way   190
The Next Chapter   192
The Working From Anywhere TagAlong   194
Acknowledgements   195
End Notes   200
Endorsements   204

| Introduction

"You only live once, but if you do it right, once is enough."

Mae West

"Live as if you were to die tomorrow. Learn as if you were to live forever."

Mahatma Gandhi

"Happiness, not in another place but this place…not for another hour, but this hour."

Walt Whitman

"Carpe diem. Seize the day, boys. Make your lives extraordinary."

Robin Williams

These are just a few of the many inspirational quotes from inspirational people about living life today, the last of which, Carpe Diem is my life mantra.

Most of us would like to think we do this, could do it, might do it, if only life and business didn't get in the way. The reality is we haven't been conditioned to live to seize the day, let alone much else. The conventional way of living has trained and conditioned us to work hard and save hard during the prime of our life so we can then have the 'freedom' to live life to the fullest in retirement.

This way of thinking has been passed down through generations so that we focus on the future rather than living in the present.

Bucket lists are banned in my books! Why? Most people believe they'll get to tick everything off once they retire, but the reality is that although by retirement age you may well have the time and money, very often health lets you down.

You ought to stop waiting for the magic day when all the stars are aligned, and start making time for life now. It's time to start doing those things on that list - **TODAY.**

| Why I wrote this book?

Stuck waiting in yet another airport, I picked up Tim Ferris' book, The 4-Hour Work Week. The tagline - Escape the 9-5, live anywhere and join the new rich - attracted my attention. While not a revolutionary concept, the notion of being able to live anywhere and work less suddenly hit home. Though my conference business was successful, it dawned on me that I was trapped in it and tied to my desk when I wasn't travelling between events.

I knew I wanted more, to live more; I needed to seize the day and embrace the working from anywhere concept.

Making the transition didn't happen overnight, but I knew that for anything at all to happen, I just had to start. I made it my mission to work out how I could do more of the things I loved — travelling and cycling — but still run my business and feel successful.

Over a period of years, I tried and tested communications platforms, project management tools, collaboration tools, email programs and file storage platforms. I worked out systems and procedures and methods to allow me and my team to work effectively from anywhere.

The Working From Anywhere (WFA) concept began to unfold, and then I

put it into practice by going to the French Alps for the month of May 2013 to work from there.

It worked so well that I returned for 2 months the following year, then 3 months the next and every year after.

As friends and clients began to notice my trips to France getting longer each year, their curiosity was piqued. How is it that you're always travelling, enjoying life and yet still running a great business?

Little by little I began to teach others what I'd done and how they could do it too. I distilled the process into a 5-step system which anyone could implement, regardless of the size of their business or industry. It simply required a willingness to embrace change and the belief that life is for living now, not when you retire.

I soon realised that this was what I wanted to do, to help other people to discover what I had, it felt like it was my purpose in life. So, after 15 years in the conference business, I wound it up to focus on my purpose and WFA.Life was born.

Since then I've realised very clearly whom I want to help and how. I've learnt by listening and observing the many people on my programs.

I've looked on as these business owners discovered the connection and how transitioning their business to work from anywhere became much more than working anywhere — it became their pathway to living life **The Carpe Diem Way.**

And that's why I've written this book.

| Who is this book for?

This book is the first step in awakening the desire for a new way of being. It's the first hint that there is another way of working and living.

Which brings me to a point that I want to make very clear: this process doesn't just work for single successful men and women with an online business. It works for those with families, those with staff and those with bricks and mortar businesses. The degree to which you implement each part of the process will depend on what you choose to let go of. The common denominator for all the people I have worked with however is this: the deep desire to live more and work less while still being effective and feeling successful.

Here are just some of the businesses that have implemented the tools and strategies in the five steps in the chapters that follow:

> **Conference and event management** - this is where it all began for me. Starting in 2013, I have spent up to three months each year operating this business from the French Alps.

> **Café and local produce store** - the business owner wanted to travel to the UK and Europe to visit family for a month in 2017. She implemented these steps, left for the UK and Europe for one month and came back two months later.

Timber industry - the owner of this business with a team of 30 had a health scare which forced him to take time out. On his return, he implemented the strategies in this book and now spends up to two months at a time travelling each year.

Leadership coach with a partner and young son - went from juggling a seven-day workweek with little time for family to a four-day week with regular family time and extended holidays.

Oyster farmers - implemented the strategies in this book so they could oversee and work on their business from the Cloud whilst travelling.

Organic skincare - a business that manufactures and sells organic skincare products. Now enjoys regular caravan trips away with a young family, working from anywhere and selling their products wholesale to stores as they travel.

Photography - a mother with a young family built up the business now employing four team members, and systemised it so she does not need to be there all the time.

So you don't need an online business to work from anywhere and live *The Carpe Diem Way*. If this diverse range of businesses can do it, then chances are you can too.

| How this book works

This book provides the reasons why and the benefits of transitioning your business to operate from anywhere, at anytime and on any device. It also gives clear and concise action steps. I recommend you read right through first, maybe skimming over the step by step actions for now. This will give you the big picture that will make implementing the steps much easier.

I have also allocated some space and prompts for notes along the way. These are your spaces, your opportunity to commit to paper what is important to you.

The case studies will show you how The Carpe Diem Way works in real life.

I share the real-life journey that led me—not totally intentionally—to understand that there is no such thing as work-life balance. There is only life. I share how transitioning my successful conference and event management business to operate from anywhere not only changed the way I work, it changed the way I live.

I was nearing the empty nesting stage of my life when I started my transformation, but you don't need to wait until then. There is no perfect starting point, and I'm going to prove this to you by sharing the story of Justine, a successful business owner with a young child.

An ex-corporate turned sole trader, Justine thought she had it all worked out, until she realised that by juggling a young child, contract work, board responsibility and a coaching business, she'd fallen back into the 'busy means successful' trap.

Going from a seven-day workweek with little time for her family to a four-day workweek with flexibility has transformed life for Justine. She now chooses when to work, where to work, and when to make time for family and her own wellbeing. But, equally important, Justine overcame the guilt that comes with making these big life changes. Trust me, you'll face mindset challenges, and I'm going to help you with those too.

Allow me to share with you the 5 steps that these people put in place to make it happen:

Step 1 - The Foundation

Step 2 - Anywhere, anytime, any device

Step 3 - Getting the processes out of your head

Step 4 – Day-to-day operations from anywhere

Step 5 - Make TIME for LIFE.

You can customise each step to fit your personal situation.

But it's not only about business systems. By the time you get to the end of the book, you'll be on your own path to living **The Carpe Diem Way.**

Let's get started. Seize this day!

Section 1 |

Gather ye rosebuds while ye may,
Old Time is still a-flying;
And this same flower that smiles today
Tomorrow will be dying.

The glorious lamp of heaven, the sun,
The higher he's a-getting,
The sooner will his race be run,
And nearer he's to setting.

That age is best which is the first,
When youth and blood are warmer;
But being spent, the worse, and worst
Times still succeed the former.

Then be not coy, but use your time,
And while ye may, go marry;
For having lost but once your prime,
You may forever tarry.

Robert Herrick, 1591 - 1674

| Why The Carpe Diem Way?

"'Gather ye rosebuds while ye may'. The Latin term for that sentiment is Carpe Diem. Now who knows what that means? Seize the day. 'Gather ye rosebuds while ye may'. Why does the writer use these lines? Because we are food for worms, lads. Because, believe it or not, each and every one of us in this room is one day gonna stop breathing, turn cold, and die."

This comes from the famous scene in the classic film Dead Poets Society starring Robin Williams.

Robin Williams, playing inspiring but unorthodox English teacher John Keating, has this conversation with his male prep school students after taking them out of the classroom.

He has them first discuss the phrase carpe diem "seize the day" they then approach glass display cases filled with trophies, footballs and team pictures. He emphasises that they should make the most of their short lives.

This movie and this scene had an almost subliminal effect on me as, unbeknownst to me at the time, they would become a big part of my life.

The loss of a mentor and friend

When I was 38 I lost a good friend and mentor. We were the same age and

we had our whole lives ahead of us. Russell was a kind, generous, happy-go-lucky man who loved sport, in particular cricket. He had it in his sights to travel to England to watch an Ashes Test at Lords one day.

Russell was my boss at the time, the owner of a local supermarket in partnership with his wife Pam, brother Ian and his wife Kaye. They had done the hard yards early to build the business, and there were tough times along the way, but they got through them and built up a very successful business. Problem was, it was a seven-day-a-week business, long hours, hard work and very little in the way of time off.

They had a plan though: they would build the business up to a point where they could sell it for a reasonable profit and move onto a different lifestyle that didn't involve a seven-day-a-week job. Russell would then be able to realise his dream of going to an Ashes Test at the hallowed ground that is Lords.

I still remember the day when I and my fellow managers were called into their office for a meeting. The conversation that followed took everyone by surprise. Russell had a kidney disease, and the only solution was a kidney transplant.

We were gobsmacked. We hadn't seen that one coming.

In the short term it meant regular dialysis and some big changes to his lifestyle while he went onto the waiting list for a compatible donor.

Several months later, big news: they had found a compatible donor and suddenly Russell was off to Sydney for the big op that would give him back his life.

Everyone's spirits lifted in anticipation of a successful outcome.

Unfortunately it was not to be.

The operation went well, but the recovery not so well. Unfortunately Russell's body rejected the kidney.

Russell died aged 38.

Ironically, the supermarket was sold that same year, a plan that was already in place before Russell's illness.

It was then that I decided to make the most of every day, plan for the short term and not dream of what I would do in the distant future.

It was then that I vowed to seize the day every single day.

Has a similar story played out in your life?

Unfortunately, it's not uncommon. Many people either don't make it to retirement or make it there in poor health.

Are you willing to take that risk?

If not, read on and let's look at *The Carpe Diem Way* of living life.

"If somebody offers you an amazing opportunity but you are not sure you can do it, say yes – then learn how to do it later!"

Richard Branson

ANDY'S STORY

The start of a Carpe Diem life

"Yeah, not a problem," I said. "I'll put something together," even though I had absolutely no experience or any idea of what was involved in putting together a national conference and trade show for 200+ business operators.

How did I get there?

Back in September 1999, a business opportunity arose at about the same time as the supermarket I had been working in as bottle shop manager was changing hands. I took the leap into buying a retail travel agency, something I knew absolutely nothing about, but the entrepreneur in me thought, really, how hard could it be?

Well it was hard. The hours were long and the margins small. Hard work for very little return. Little did I know that a significant carpe diem moment was about to change the course of my business life.

Steve, a local businessman and board member of a Fuel Industry Association, asked if I would be interested in quoting on their next conference.

I said yes. It didn't matter to me that I had absolutely zero experience in that particular field.

I did the research, made some calls, reached out to some potential conference venues, and put it all together as a PowerPoint presentation. I was as ready as I was ever going to be to pitch to the next Caltex National Distributors Association board meeting.

Walking into Caltex headquarters, signing in and collecting my security badge, going down the polished corridors to the boardroom, I felt somewhat intimidated. I had no idea if what I'd prepared was up to the

expected standard, let alone if it could stand out enough to win the day. That said, there was nothing to lose.

I'd worked hard on the proposal for a five-day conference on Hamilton Island, inclusive of flights, accommodation, conference sessions, dinners, activities, a Gala Dinner and a trade exhibition.

I explained how I would work with them to stage an exciting and memorable conference for their members, and it would be the complete package.

Then I left the big smoke feeling it was a stretch at best that I would win the contract, but I'd given it my best shot and, back home in the day-to-day craziness of a retail travel agency in Bega, I felt pretty damn proud of myself.

Three days later the phone call came: I had the gig.

Then it hit me: I'd better start working out how the hell to organise and run a conference — and fast. I went to work.

The first item on the agenda of the first planning meeting was developing a conference theme. I boldly suggested that 'carpe diem' would be a good fit based on the messages they were looking to deliver. They agreed.

As it turned out, the carpe diem theme was not only fitting for their event, it also became the mantra that would change and shape my life for the next 15 years and beyond.

I went from struggling in the highly competitive retail travel agency game in a small regional town to building a conference and event management business organising million-dollar events all around the world.

What if I had said no to that opportunity to quote on the conference? I'll never know because I chose to seize the day and work the rest out later.

| The Conventional Way

> "The biggest difference between money and time: You always know how much money you have but you never know how much time you have ...Enjoy every moment of your life."
>
> Unknown

First let's look at the conventional way we've been conditioned to live as a business owner, before we move onto the much better alternative. Let's look at life as we know it:

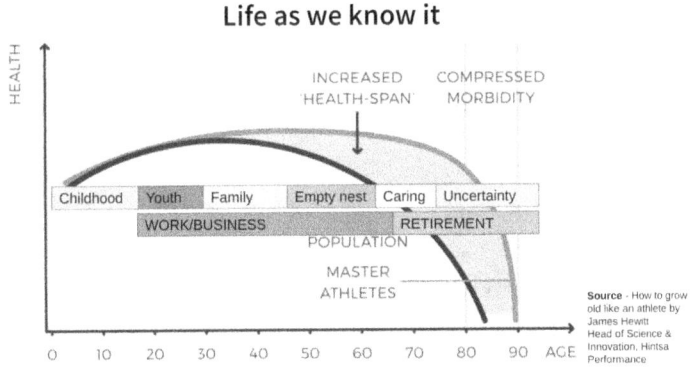

The above graph shows an indicative lifespan and healthspan, although of course these vary for each individual.

The average life expectancy for Australians is currently 81 for males and 85 for females. Of course some people live a lot longer and others, unfortunately, do not.

Life starts off in childhood, where all our needs are taken care of by our parents.

Next comes youth, when our education begins. The biggest demand on our time is the six-hour school day, five days a week with a little bit of time supposedly set aside for homework.

We get to enjoy four lots of school holidays, a total of 10+ weeks, every year, time that we don't think too much about. It's just what life is at the time. It's also a time of life that our parents like to remind us is the "best years of your life", a statement that we usually disregard as we can't imagine them ever having been our age.

We complete high school and are faced with our first major decisions. Do we continue down the education path to university, or take the TAFE path or seek out a trade apprenticeship.

What course do we pick and what marks do we need?

The other option is to bypass further education and get out there and join the workforce.

Eventually all roads lead to being gainfully employed in some capacity.

How exciting, we have grown up. We have money to spend, and everything is looking good in our now adult world.

Wait a minute though, what do you mean we have to be at work for eight hours every day, sometimes longer if things are busy? Gone are the six weeks off over Christmas and the other three holiday breaks a year.

We now have to work for a full 12 months before we can apply for our four weeks' annual leave. Do we take it all at once or in mini-breaks over the next 12 months?

Then we get to the time of life where we start our own family — exciting, but also a huge commitment to time. Our career is moving along nicely, or we may have taken the leap from career to business owner.

We're now juggling work or our own business with an expanding family, school events, spending time with the kids. Time to ourselves is a thing of the past.

Hmmm, we have less time to exercise and we now watch the kids play sport rather than take part in it ourselves. Our hectic schedule sees us grabbing takeaways and eating on the run, and we start putting on a little bit of weight, losing sleep and generally feeling fatigued and unhealthy.

Then, in the blink of an eye, the first of the kids is leaving home to start their own life and career and, before we know it, we have a house without children and understand the term 'empty nest'.

Surely we'll have some more 'me' time now, but where did all those years go?

This is when we should be able to take some of those trips we've been dreaming of, but there's still the business to run. We make plans for later, for when we sell the business and retire. That's when we think we'll have the time, money and freedom to realise our travel dreams.

10-15 years should do it. "I'll work hard, keep putting as much as I can into super, and then at 67 I can really start living. I just can't wait."

As the years pass, so do friends and colleagues — people our age.

An old school friend I haven't caught up with for many years because

we've both been too busy with 'life' is nearing retirement, has bought a caravan and was all set for retirement freedom, but he's just found out he has cancer, and has to go for treatment. He's hopeful that it will all work out.

The caravanning adventure is on hold.

Think about it, we spend the majority of the prime of our life – from 18 to 67 – dreaming of and planning what we'll do in our twilight years, when our body and/or mind may or may not be up to it.

IF retirement age is 67,

AND life expectancy is 70s–80s,

WORK for 50 years to maybe enjoy 11 years?

This mindset is especially so for business owners and entrepreneurs. We go into business for ourselves because of the freedom it offers, but what happens instead is that most of us end up with a job where we work more hours, more often than not earn less money, have less time for the people that matter to us and find ourselves on a treadmill of never-ending busyness.

There are three things you need to realise your retirement dreams — and you do need all three:

1. Money
2. Time
3. Health.

Money - you've saved hard, you've sacrificed some of life's immediate pleasures and instead been diligent in adding to your superannuation. You've had to use some of your super savings to pay down your mortgage

and some other debts, but you still have enough left over to realise your dreams. The many years of hard work have paid off — you've got the *money* part covered.

Time - You no longer need to go to the office, open the shop, run the business or whatever else you've been doing for the past 40 years. *Time* is yours — you're in total control of your time, and you can do what you want when you want.

This is what you've been dreaming of — you've got the *time* part covered.

Health - Now here's the part that causes the most trouble – there are a number of scenarios that could play out here, none of which you find out about until it's too late.

1. Physical fitness and mobility
2. Your own general health
3. The health of a parent or family member.

#1 Physical fitness and mobility: Best case scenario, you get to retirement with reasonable health. You're older though, and the body ain't quite what it used to be. Those sporting injuries from your youth are starting to create aches and pains; that knee you hurt playing netball is now locking up; walking uphill is a challenge, and walking down is even worse.

If you're in your 30s or even 40s right now, these things will not even enter your mind, because at every point in life we think that this is how we'll always feel.

Next time you're out for a run, a walk on the beach or even just shopping, take the time to look around at the older and some not so old people with mobility issues. These same people were once just like you are right now: mobile, and thinking that that's how it would always be.

So right now this may not be a thing for you but, trust me, as you get older it will be, and there is no way to turn back time.

Climbing that mountain you had on your bucket list is not looking so good now. Doing it 10 years ago would've been a much better idea.

If only you could turn back time!

#2 Your own health - We all tend to take our general health for granted, but the reality is as we age our general health declines, leaving us with ailments ranging from minor to chronic.

So often the health issue happens fast, really fast. Suddenly life has to be put on hold and the only plan is one for the best means of recovery.

When chronic illness strikes unexpectedly, radically changing life or, the worst-case scenario, taking a life, it's a shock. Especially when it's in our own circle of family, mates and colleagues. We all know someone it has happened to.

You would think planning to retire early was a good game plan, but even that doesn't always pan out.

I hosted an FB Live show called *The Carpe Diem Conversation Show*, where I interviewed business owners with a carpe diem story to share.

One interview was with Emma Rhoades:

Emma's father had what seemed like a great plan: he would work hard, dedicate his days to building up the business, and make some sacrifices in the short term. He would then retire early and travel before he got too old.

Unfortunately it didn't work out that way.

> "My life changed dramatically when my father passed away, and he was only 54 years old.

"He had worked all his life. He had created a business and he'd set it up for his retirement. Both my Mum and Dad were going to go travelling.

"They were going to do some more socialising and really live the next chapter of their lives. Unfortunately, he didn't quite make it. At 52 he retired, at 53 he was diagnosed with cancer, and then at 54 he passed away."

It was a tragic time for Emma and her family — it was life-changing.

There is a golden lining to Emma's story. Determined to learn from the experience, Emma took action, putting in place changes to allow her to live life now, not some day off in the future. That proved an important pivot in her life and she hasn't looked back since.

"So for me, my whole life just shifted and everything became about living for now, no more waiting.

"After we shifted our family back home to Coffs Harbour, I set up a photography business, determined to be around my young kids and drop them off and pick them up from school. I needed to fit in with that. Photography is a passion of mine, so I started building that business.

"From the moment I knew my business could be systemised, I went for it. Two short years later and I had a team of four, a physical studio space and was working weddings up and down the Coast. We moved everything online and I didn't even have to see my photographers, although of course I still did because I wanted to!

"The business was operating without me and I was also fulfilling my dream helping other business owners to live the same life, heading to the beach with the kids after school, and playing golf every Friday afternoon.

#3 The health of a parent or family member

You may reach retirement with your health intact, but there's another health risk that is not often considered — it doesn't enter most people's minds.

As you age, so do your partner, children, parents and siblings. As your parents age there's a good chance they will increasingly need your care and attention. The unknown is when, whether they or you and your siblings can afford a first or second choice care solution and what other options are available. Whether by choice or necessity your priorities change, and your retirement may not be what you planned.

I have a friend who is a keen cyclist and adventurer, an enthusiast for the French language and the French village lifestyle. He had a clear retirement plan: he would work just another few years, and then retire and head over to France to spend extended periods practising his French and immersing himself in a small French village.

He just wanted to work a few more years to make sure there was plenty in his superannuation fund — just another few years would do it.

He finally made it to retirement. He now had the freedom and the money to realise his dream of being a part-time Frenchman.

BUT it didn't quite work out that way. Just before he retired his mother became ill with Alzheimer's disease. He wanted and needed to be with his mother as well as his elderly father to support them through this challenging time,.

Consequently he had two of the three things needed to realise his dreams: he had money and his own health, but due to his mother's ill health he lost (willingly) his time, caring and supporting both elderly parents.

After a long battle his mother passed away, leaving his elderly father on his own. The French dreams have been put on hold for now as his father needs his care and attention.

In the meantime, a frustration: he is on a waiting list for a hip replacement, so his dream of cycling in France may only ever be a dream.

Maybe holding off to top the superannuation up wasn't such a great idea as he now only has one of the three things needed to realise his dreams.

If only he could turn back time.

All through our working lives it's drummed into us by our parents, our teachers, our financial advisers and the government that we need to build a massive nest egg to make sure we don't run out of funds when we retire.

Building wealth for our later years is important, but my question is whether there is too much focus on building up a retirement nest egg for the future and not enough on making **TIME** for **LIFE** now?

Which would you rather run out of first?

Money or life?

There you have it: the conventional way we've been conditioned to live as a business owner, and live life in general, has some serious flaws.

There is another way you can live life as a business owner, a way that gives you the opportunity to do the things you are dreaming of doing in retirement and not putting them off until later, but doing these things now. This alternative also gives you the opportunity to take control of your days, freeing up time to do the other things you enjoy, fitting your work around life rather than your life around work.

I call it living **The Carpe Diem Way**.

Whether you're an owner of a well established, successful business that is dependent on you always being there, or you're in the earlier growth stages of building a business with seemingly not enough hours in any day, either way your business is your life. If you're missing out on spending quality time with your partner, family, friends, your health and wellness could be suffering, and if you no longer have time to do the other things in life that you enjoy, then '**The Carpe Diem Way**' is for you.

I'm sharing my insights in this book because I was in the 'let's wait till I retire to live my life' mode until 2012 when I had to reassess.

I was living this life that we have all been conditioned to. I had built a very successful business and I was focused on building up enough funds to retire on, one day. The only problem was that it meant that I was working long hours and weekends. I was travelling constantly, living out of hotel rooms and convention centres, too busy to spend time with my family, friends or even myself. The business became my life.

SUMMARY AND ACTIONS

Making it to retirement age, cashing in the Super, selling the business and starting to live our dreams is a way of life with some serious flaws. Just because your parents did it that way doesn't mean you have to.

Once your health takes a dive, there go your choices, your plans, your dreams.

Planning for an early retirement can be a good idea, but not if it comes at the expense of living your best life every day.

Take Action:

- Ditch the bucket list or any other 'I'll do this someday' list. If you want to do something, big or small, schedule it, book it in, commit to it, do it.

- Go and get that general medical check-up you've been putting off. Chances are you service your car more often than yourself. Acknowledge the known issues, face up to their potential to put limits on your future, plan accordingly. Living an unhealthy life? Do something about it.

- Consider the implications of a change in health of your aging parents.

- Listen to the interview with Emma Rhoades, an inspiring account of building a business that could run without her, helping other photographers do what they wanted to do, and fulfilling her dream of being able to support and help other business owners to live the same life. (link to this can be found at *https://wfa.life/resources*)

STOP!

Make TIME for LIFE.

I know you're keen to get through the book so you can put the five steps into action.

But it's not just about taking action in your business.

We all need a **WHY** to keep us on track when making life changes.

So throughout the book I've given you blank pages with questions.

Answering them will help you figure out **WHY** the hell you should do the five steps.

You don't have to want to live in France for three months each year for this to work for you.

Your **WHY** is your own and should be the driver for you to make changes.

It takes time to figure it out. It may change along the way.

Your notes. Your **WHY.** Your life.

Your chance to start living the Carpe Diem Way.

| My Carpe Diem Way

Book readers grab a pen. On the ebook? Hit the notes tab.
Find a quiet place and reflect on what you've read so far.

Now I want you to think about what is important to you - people, places, beliefs, the things you do.

Start writing. List everything that's important to you.

| THE **CARPE DIEM** WAY | MY CARPE DIEM WAY

_____
_____
_____
_____
_____
_____
_____
_____
_____
_____
_____
_____
_____
_____
_____
_____
_____
_____
_____
_____
_____
_____

> "Regardless of WHAT we do in our lives, our WHY—our driving purpose, cause or belief—never changes."
>
> Simon Sinek

ANDY'S STORY

When life throws curveballs

Fast forward 11 years to 2012.

In that time I had built a very successful conference and event management business.

The events had long lead times, 12-18 months of preparation and planning. We arranged everything: flights from all around Australia to the overseas destination, transport, accommodation, conference sessions, keynote speakers, activities, tours, gala dinners and post-conference extension tours.

It was an enormously successful business, both enjoyable and profitable, but it meant working hard, seven days a week at times — long days, time away from family and really no time for life outside the business.

That's okay, I thought, I can live it up later.

I spent a fair amount of time travelling, hanging around at airports, long hours on long flights. I often picked up a book at the airport bookshop before boarding my flight, because I had no time to find one before I got to the airport. It was one of these books that, unbeknown to me at the time, would change my life forever.

This book, The 4-Hour Work Week by Timothy Ferris, was about the concept of spending less time working in your business. I didn't at the time, and still don't believe, there is such a thing as a four-hour workweek, but the concept of systemising your business so you could operate it working from anywhere got me thinking maybe I could do this with my business.

There was only one way to find out. I made the big decision to transition

my conference and event management business to operate 'working from anywhere'.

Life works in mysterious ways, and life throws curveballs when you least expect it. I was about to get the opportunity to put the work from anywhere concept into real life practice sooner than I thought.

My life was about to change. I became a single man again. It was a very tough and dark time. There were times when my head was anywhere but in my business, but I really needed to 'be there' as I was only three months away from one of the biggest conference events I'd ever organised.

This sudden change in circumstances left me with only two choices: I could dwell on my misfortune, spiral into self-pity and watch as my successful business went to ruin or I could just get on with it.

I decided on the latter, put my head down and worked hard to make sure the upcoming event would be one of the best.

It also presented me with another once in a lifetime opportunity: to invite my eldest daughter Aleisha to work with me at the event. The event itself and the pre- and post- conference extension tours were an amazing success, Aleisha worked with me as though she'd been in the game her whole life and we had a fabulous team on the ground in Vancouver.

By the time I joined the group for the post-conference seven-night Alaska cruise, I was absolutely exhausted. The previous months and full-on pace of running the five-day event had caught up with me, I went straight to my cabin and collapsed into a deep sleep.

Finally I had time on my own to think, to ponder where to from here, to put more thought into the working from anywhere concept.

It also gave me the space to think about what I love doing. I'm a crazy keen

cyclist. I'd been to France back in 2010 with a group of mates to cycle and watch a few stages of the Tour de France. I really enjoyed my few days in the French Alps and promised myself that I'd go back 'one day'.

It may have been the sea air, too many cocktails on the deck or just the time I had to think more clearly, but it was during that cruise that I decided to turn that 'one day' into 'some day soon'. I decided to step up my decision to transition my conference business to work from anywhere and fully commit to making it happen.

No sooner had I returned from the conference than I'd booked flights to France and rented an apartment in a small village in the French Alps for the whole month of May 2013.

What I thought was the biggest disaster in my life was turning into the opportunity of a lifetime.

Section 2

| The Mindset Shift:
The Carpe Diem Way to live life as a business owner

Imagine if:

- You could do the things you dream about doing when you retire, now. Go to faraway places to enjoy some slow travel, hook up the caravan for three months to explore, or simply have guilt-free time for family, friends and doing the things you love

- You could remove yourself from the daily grind, meet new people and discover places unknown while your business is still operating

- You could do all or any of this without retiring or selling your business

- As you travel, or just live life on your terms, your business continues to pay you an income, continues to contribute to your superannuation

- Every day you felt more healthy, less stressed and more in love with life.

This is not a holiday, it's not work — it's life, it's **The Carpe Diem Way.**

Is this really possible?

Yes it is.

Feeling overwhelmed by the possibilities? Don't be.

I've done it. And this book will see you through the process step by step.

Before we launch into the detail or start taking action, I want you to take a moment to take this in:

These are the three things that will set you up for success on your shift to living *The Carpe Diem Way*.

1. The right tools
2. Some simple systems
3. A mindset shift.

The right tools — there are plenty out there, and more being created every minute of the day. How do you find the right ones for your business? There are so many that seem to do the same thing. Which ones are best and how do you keep up with all the changes?

You already have so much technology, you seem to spend most of your day going from one app to the other and not getting any real work done.

I've been there and done that. I've lost count of the number of tech tools, platforms and apps I've signed up for, paid for, learned how to use, used a little or a lot, only to move on when the next shiny object in the form of a new best yet tech tool comes along.

I've spent the greater part of many a day jumping from one productivity tool to another, without getting any real work done. This has been me for many, many years — the latest discovery was always going to be the one.

But while I have often rued the number of hours I wasted, after a while I

realised that they weren't really wasted at all.

I eventually came across one platform that included most of the tools I needed, all in one place, a suite of tools. This very same platform also integrated with a few other essentials to provide me with a very much simplified toolkit.

The other reason it wasn't really wasted time was because I spent all those hours and hours and lots of money finding, learning, signing up for, testing, discarding and moving to the next thing, so you don't need to.

I've narrowed down the list significantly for you, and I'll explain as we work through the five steps to **The Carpe Diem Way**.

Then there are the **simple systems**

The challenge for us as business owners is we have built the business and the processes that make the business work, but the problem is that most of the how-to-do stuff is in our head. Sure, other people can do much of it once they've been trained, but there are still some things that "only I know how to do."

It takes time to train new people in our business, to pass the knowledge from our head to theirs. Then you get them to train other people, but that only means they transfer knowledge from their head to the next person's.

And so the cycle continues in a very time-consuming way.

The challenge of course is that, just like a whispering game, some parts are changed in translation and everyone does each process just a little differently, so there is no consistency.

The solution is to get this knowledge, process or procedure out of your and everyone else's head and into a system that anyone can access *from anywhere, at anytime and on any device.*

The aim of the game is to set your business up so that any and all of the people in your business can do the majority of the tasks, processes and procedures with very little intervention, and without taking up someone else's time – actually your time.

This strategy to implement simple systems has been proven to save time, create consistency, increase profitability and, as a big bonus, make everyone's life easier.

Then, last but not least, actually in most cases the biggest challenge is the **shift in mindset.**

Breaking the conditioning of generations is not easy, and making changes to how you work and live is uncomfortable at best.

These changes range from learning new technology to moving away from working in the eight-hour blocks the industrial world has created for us.

Most business owners who come to me for help say things like "I'm the only one that can do X" or "I'm too nervous to trust someone else to do Y" or "My customers expect me to do Z for them."

I get it. I've been there. After so many years of doing it all, it's hard to let go.

I have run numerous programs for business owners over the years that combined cloud technology online tutorials, one-on-one sessions and Mastermind sessions.

Program members have different levels of skills and needs for the technology part of the program. Some get there quicker than others, but the biggest challenge by far for everyone is the change of mindset.

That's where the Mastermind sessions came to the fore, and where people realise that they are not the only ones struggling to break away from the norm to the shift in mindset that is necessary.

A six-month mastermind and mentoring program, finished with the participants putting it all into practice at a seven-day Carpe Diem retreat in the French Alps. The mindset challenges made up the greater part of the conversations, and there were a tear or two as a result, so it was quite an emotional week.

Putting the tools and simple systems in place actually assists in shifting this mindset, but it is still an enormous challenge for most people.

The other challenge is guilt, the feeling that we are expected to do X, Y and Z, and should lead by example rather than delegate responsibility.

Of course the exact opposite is true. The more you delegate responsibility, the more empowered your team becomes, the more ideas and solutions flow and you develop a much more happy and productive team.

Which of course leads to happier, more contented customers, so consequently more sales and profit for the business.

I think now is a good time to bring Justine into the story as someone who came to me with what she thought was the need to upskill herself on the latest productivity technology. As it turned out, that was only a part of the problem and technology wasn't the golden bullet, but it was part of the solution.

Changing her mindset brought the biggest result by far.

This is where Justine was at when she came to me for help:

> "So I had a very successful corporate career that started in hospitality, but I spent most of my career in human resources, working at the executive level. I really loved working. I travelled a lot, I had a great life, and I didn't think I would have a family.
>
> "And then I decided to have a baby and Nash came along. I was

> preparing to go back to work when I realised that perhaps my old life was not going to fit my new needs.
>
> "Traditionally, because I managed large teams and worked in bigger organisations, my roles included a lot of travel, and it just wasn't going to work."

Justine decided to create her own leadership business, a business that would satisfy her financial and purpose needs. She thought that creating her own business and being her own boss would provide her with the freedom and flexibility to nurture her family and also satisfy her passion and purpose.

Leaders Change Room was born, and it soon developed and grew to be a very successful business. The only problem was it became a seven-day-a-week job rather than the business that promised the freedom and flexibility Justine was seeking for herself and her family.

The roadblock for Justine was thinking that as a solo business operator she had to do everything herself. Previously she had had support staff, but now she believed she was too small to engage outside help.

Her mindset was stuck on believing that's what a small business is: you need to do everything yourself.

> "I had teams and support staff to handle that for me. You know, IT departments who could help out, and finance departments.
>
> "And then when you start on your own, it's all you. I do not love admin, and it really drains my energy.
>
> "And I found that I was spending most of my weekends with a laptop open somewhere in the house, trying to get it done in-between, or waiting for Nash to go to bed and staying up till midnight to try and

get it done so I could be present with clients in the morning. And that was a real juggle for me, and I didn't love it. Gotta be honest."

It was at this point that Justine joined the Work From Anywhere Mastermind & Mentoring Program I was running at the time.

The "It's just me, I'm not big enough" was just one of the mindset myths that were to be busted on her journey to *The Carpe Diem Way.*

There are five powerful steps to transitioning your business to operate from *anywhere, at anytime and on any device.*

The very same five powerful steps that Justine took on her journey from a seven-day workweek with little time for her family to a four-day workweek with flexibility and the opportunity to make **TIME** for **LIFE** for herself and her family.

There is more to this than learning how to work remotely. You will uncover life opportunities along the way that you didn't know existed.

This is all really hard to imagine, but I've seen it happen with business owners on every program. The time frame is different for each individual, but there comes a point when the penny drops.

Read on, as I share these five powerful steps and Justine's journey through them.

✱ SUMMARY AND ACTIONS

It is possible to:

- Do the things you dream about doing when you retire now. Enjoy some slow travel to faraway places, hook up the caravan for three months to explore, or simply have guilt-free time for family, friends and doing the things you love

- Remove yourself from the daily grind, meet new people and discover places unknown while your business is still operating

- Do all or any of the above without retiring or selling your business

- Travel, or just live life on your own terms while your business continues to pay you an income, continues to contribute to your superannuation

- Feel more healthy, less stressed and more in love with life.

You need three things to live The Carpe Diem Way : the right tools, some simple systems, a mindset shift.

Take Action:

- Go back to your list of 'everything that is important to you' that you wrote on "My Carpe Diem" page. Read it again. Don't lose sight of your 'why?'.

STOP!

Make TIME for LIFE.

Time for a reality check.

How much time do you really spend

with the people who count in your life

doing the things you love

in places that are special to you

or delivering on your beliefs?

It's your life. Your notes. Your TIME.

Your chance to start living the Carpe Diem Way.

| My Carpe Diem Way

List the people and things that are important to you again here, but now add the amount of time you spend with each one.

This can be the average per day, week, month — whatever fits with the people or activity.

(You may want to check in with someone on your list to see if they agree!)

| THE **CARPE DIEM** WAY | MY CARPE DIEM WAY

"It's being here now that's important. There's no past and there's no future. Time is a very misleading thing. All there is, ever, is the now. We can gain experience from the past, but we can't relive it; and we can hope for the future, but we don't know if there is one."

George Harrison

ANDY'S STORY

I packed my bag, my bike and my laptop - May 2013

2013 was a pretty big year. We had some major events on the go: a study tour in Seoul and Tokyo for a fuel industry group, a five-day conference for 100+ Caltex distributors in Port Douglas, a three-day event at Homebush including a big Gala Dinner event for 250 people and, to top it off, a 14-day cycling tour in France. We were also managing the bookings for my sister's Sharing Bali Retreats, and then we had my own event, the annual Bandanna Day Bike charity event to raise funds for young people living with cancer.

And I was leaving to spend the full month of May on the other side of the world? What was I thinking?

I got to work transitioning into my working-from-anywhere mode. I moved all my files off the server and into the Cloud. Back then this was Microsoft Skydrive and a platform called Sharepoint. As long as I had an internet connection, I now had complete access to all my business files from anywhere.

I moved from a desktop accounting package to the online version, giving me complete control over the financial side of my business on a daily basis.

I signed up for Skype phone numbers for the business. The call quality wasn't fantastic, but it was a much better solution than redirecting calls to mobiles, which was both inconvenient and very expensive. I had unlimited calls from and to almost everywhere in the world for $128.00/year, an absolute bargain at the time.

If this was going to work, I thought it best to get some practice in, so I started working outside the office for at least one day a week, testing to

make sure I could access everything as though I was overseas, as though I was already hanging out in the French Alps.

Kaycee and I used Skype to chat, tested working on documents and conference delegate lists together online, set up protocols around how we would communicate, put some simple systems in place for working on conference lists to make sure we didn't overwrite each other's work, and set up tasks in an online project and task management tool.

We even tested using Skype for video calls to each other.

At this point I must give credit to Kaycee, who not only accepted my crazy shift in work practices, but embraced it.

Testing, 1...2...3... yes, everything seems to work.

My flights were booked, my little apartment in Allemont, a small village in the French Alps, confirmed, I'd booked a car, got myself a global SIM card, loaded up a travel card with Euro and I'd even managed to line up someone to teach me French during my stay.

It was time to pack my bike, bag, laptop, mobile phone, chargers, adapters and other technology bits and pieces.

I've got this, I kept saying to myself. It was time to go to the airport.

Sitting in the lounge with a glass of champagne, I thought about the decisions I'd made that had me about to board a plane to experience life on my own in another country with minimal language competency.

I reflected on my mantra, carpe diem. I was living my life in the present, and I didn't want to defer living my best life until later.

Yeah, I can do this…

Let the adventure begin…

Touching down in Lyon, I was focused, excited and organised. I picked up my bike from oversize baggage, breezed through customs, found the free shuttle bus for the car rental — too easy. Renault collected.

So now how do you change the GPS language from French to English? Didn't think about that.

Once sorted, I was off down the motorway on the right-hand side of the road, a very strange sensation, especially with cars whizzing either side at the 130km/h speed limit. Steady as she goes. I've got this. The roundabouts were a particular challenge and there were times when I did the loop more than once to make sure I took the right exit.

As I sped down the motorway, the feeling of excitement with a touch of anxiety was like nothing I'd ever experienced before.

Passing through Grenoble after just over an hour was another level of excitement and trepidation. The mountains rose around me, then the motorway gave way to more basic two-way roads that narrowed as I started climbing. Part of me was focused on driving, but my mind was on another track . . . I'd actually left, taken the leap, trusted myself to make this work.

Two hours later I arrived without incident at Le Génépi, my home in the Alps for the next month.

It took all of two seconds to realise my first challenge: Eric, my host, didn't speak much English and I spoke even less French. Thankfully Eric's wife Griet came to the rescue with her very good grasp of English.

The next challenge came as I opened the door to find a very, very basic French village-style apartment that was the size of the lounge in my four-bedroom home. I vividly remember thinking have I made a massive mistake here?

For the past dozen years or so nothing in my life had been remotely basic. I owned a big home with some spaces that never got used, and enjoyed 5-star accommodation at the conference events I managed. Le Génépi was such a contrast to what I was used to.

Maybe it was the fatigue of the long journey, but I was feeling emotional. I'm used to spending time outside my comfort zone, but this was next level. You know what? I thought to myself, I'm here now, I can't do anything about it. Suck it up and seize the day.

I distracted myself from my temporary bout of anxiety by unpacking, putting my bike together and setting up my humble abode.

I needed supplies, so it was back in the car in search of the local supermarket.

WOW, not what I was expecting! The supermarket felt huge, and the range of fresh produce was like nothing I had seen before: baguettes, baguettes, bread and more baguettes, meat pre-packaged and a butcher counter, poultry of all varieties, fresh seafood on ice on an open table, a massive deli with more varieties of cheese than I'd ever seen before in my life, and fruit and vegetables that looked more home-grown than mass produced (the French don't expect fruit and vegetables to be the perfect shape like we do. Instead they are fresh and more on the ripe side).

It took a while to gather what I needed into my trolley. Much of the time was spent trying to read labels using my new best friend Google translate. Then it was off to the checkout, where I was about to learn lessons on the difference between how supermarkets work in France compared to Australia.

Lesson #1 - checkout operator waving my bags of fruit and veg at me, and pointing back to the fruit and veg area. Apparently you need to weigh and

price label your own fresh produce. They don't have scales at the checkout like we do at home.

Lesson #2 - France was a long way ahead of us. You need to bring your own bags or purchase reusable ones at the checkout.

Lesson #3 - The checkout operator is comfortably positioned and seated to scan your goods, and that's it. Packing your bags is not part of their job. That's on you.

An observation rather than a lesson: the French are not queue averse. The checkout operator was in no hurry. There was no rush to pay and move on. The people in the queue were not agitated and impatient. Everyone was relaxed. There was no calling up more operators as soon as there were more than two people in the queue.

It took me 2½ hours to buy two bags of groceries and spend 50 euros in the supermarket, but it was an experience I'll never forget. Sometimes it's the little things.

By the end of the day I was all set, unpacked, bike together, shopping done, food in the cupboards. It must be time to take the cork out of that bottle of French wine I picked up at the supermarket. Time for a little celebration.

Sitting on the deck, looking up at the imposingly beautiful mountains, enjoying a baguette, cheese, French wine and listening to Edith Piaf I had one thought...

Yes, this is really happening.

Carpe Diem.

Step 1 - The Foundation

> "I have to be there to answer the questions that only I know the answer to, to do the tasks that only I know how to do."

Having to be there is one of the most common barriers that prevents most successful business owners from spending more time living life outside of their business.

The problem is, most business owners don't start by building a foundation that allows them to bring other people in.

Bestselling author Michael Gerber doesn't pull any punches on his views about this:

> "If your business depends on you, you don't own a business—you have a job. And it's the worst job in the world because you're working for a lunatic!"

Gerber put business systemisation on the map with his bestselling book The E-Myth. In 2011 this book was named the number 1 business book of all time by The Wall Street Journal.

I'm an absolute fan of this book. It is another of the books that has shaped the way I work and the way I live my life.

Gerber explains that in order for a company or business to thrive, it must move beyond relying on the business owner's only role in the business as a technician. Gerber uses the franchise model to demonstrate how to create a business that operates without the business owner. "Franchises are prototype businesses that are operated in terms of well-documented systems, i.e. there are manuals describing in minute detail how to run the business." Gerber argues that business owners should spend time creating a business that can run by itself, without their presence, and that this is achieved through business systemisation.

Think of a foundation as the platform that supports the other parts, moving or static.

You can't add a foundation to a house after you've built it. Your car wouldn't go anywhere with just a motor; it needs a chassis (foundation) for the moving parts to work.

Often what happens is, as businesses grow the moving parts (the people) are added, but then they realise that there is no structure (foundation) for them.

Most business owners build their business organically, starting off small, growing and adapting. They work out how to do stuff, then refine and improve, learn as they go.

The only plan they have is a plan to grow the business. Not much thought is put into how many people will work there or how they will be trained to operate the key components of the business.

The business owner knows every aspect of the business because they created it. They know where to find the files and information because they designed the file system based on what works for them. They're accountable for everything because that's what they're used to.

As the small business grows, so does the amount of information the owner needs to run it. The files containing operational business information are organised more like a rabbit warren: a series of folders, sub-folders, sub-sub-folders, sub-sub-sub-folders and then finally the files.

Then there's the challenge of where the actual files are physically stored: files end up on individual laptops, external storage devices and thumb drives that are only accessible by the individual who saved the file.

The end result being that some people have access to some of the business data but not everything they may need to do their job. Files may be shared by email or thumb drives, but it's time-consuming and confusing, and files get duplicated, overwritten or lost forever.

The organisation may have a file server or they may have moved to cloud storage. Bravo, good move. The problem is that everyone thinks differently about how to name a file and which folder it should be stored in, duplication happens, there is more confusion and time is wasted. End result? A nightmare for the owner to find a file, let alone anyone else.

And then there is the technology — yet another thing that requires the owner's attention and promises more efficient business operations that could free up their time. But somehow technology gets added ad hoc. One team member comes across a great app and starts using it, another finds a different one and gives that a go. Before long you have multiple apps in your business that all do the same thing.

Cloud technology and the productivity tools that work with it do allow us to operate more effectively, but only if someone collaborates with the team and is accountable for what gets implemented and where.

Even though the team has grown, the owner still needs to oversee every area of the business because there are no defined key areas of accountability

to allow delegation of responsibility. There is no foundation.

The Accountability Map

Traditionally in larger organisations this foundation has been called the organisation chart. I found this definition:

"An organisational structure defines how activities such as task allocation, coordination, and supervision are directed toward the achievement of organisational aims."

At WFA we call it an *Accountability Map.*

This is an important step. You may not think so right now, but you need to create your own *Accountability Map* before you go any further.

You can pick your own tools to brainstorm this one: a piece of paper, whiteboard, a google doc — whatever works for you, but make sure you document the end result.

OR you can use my free template to create your Accountability Map. Download this template at *https://wfa.life/resources*

Business name - Accountability Map

```
                        ┌─────────────────┐
                        │ BUSINESS OWNER  │
                        │      WHO?       │
                        └─────────────────┘
```

| OPERATIONS WHO? | SALES WHO? | MARKETING WHO? | TECHNOLOGY WHO? | MANAGEMENT WHO? | FINANCE WHO? | HUMAN RESOURCES WHO? |

File Storage Structure

| OPERATIONS | SALES | MARKETING | TECHNOLOGY | MANAGEMENT | FINANCE | HUMAN RESOURCES |

Project and Task Management Platform Structure

| OPERATIONS | SALES | MARKETING | TECHNOLOGY | MANAGEMENT | FINANCE | HUMAN RESOURCES |

Standard Operating Procedures and Systems Structure

| OPERATIONS | SALES | MARKETING | TECHNOLOGY | MANAGEMENT | FINANCE | HUMAN RESOURCES |

At the top of the accountability map is the business owner. That's the easy part. Then comes the hard part.

There are three steps you need to take from here:

1. Identify the key areas of accountability in your business. The above example is just that: an example. Your business may well be different.

To get this done, ask yourself: if you had to give access to external contractors or experts where each contractor only had access to one particular area of your business, how would you define these areas?

Your accountant for instance would only need access to the finance area, not general operations or sales and marketing.

Thinking this way will set your business up for internal or external delegation of accountability.

NOTE : This needs to be done even if you have no intention of adding team members or external contractors. Believe me, there will come a time when you want to outsource something, but even if you don't, it still creates consistency for your solo operation.

2. You now need to add WHO is accountable for each of these accountability areas. You're probably thinking it's only me, why should I bother? But you must add your name to every area of accountability with the sole aim of replacing it with someone else's name sometime in the future, even if you can't see it ever happening.

3. All that's left to do now is copy and paste the rows of boxes underneath. You'll find out why later, and I guarantee an aha! moment will come your way as you implement and use the five steps.

Major supermarket chains are a great example of a solid foundation. Each store set-up is mirrored from store to store, and product layout follows the same order regardless of the size of the store.

So if you're a Woolworths shopper, no matter which store you shop at, the layout will be familiar so your shopping experience is easier.

This of course also benefits the company greatly as it allows staff to move from store to store and be able to walk in and start working without the need for costly additional training. No matter which store employees work in, every department, storage area and process is the same.

Your business is no different. If your foundation is mirrored in every area, it becomes easier for everyone to navigate. It also makes it easier to train new staff, who will only need to be introduced to the top level of the accountability map and understand that this flows through into every area of the business.

Based on this foundation, accountability is easily delegated throughout your business. As an example, the marketing team is responsible for managing the marketing files so they have their own team set-up in your project management software to manage the marketing projects and daily tasks. They are responsible for creating the SOP's that are relative to the marketing team.

Some team members may and most likely will need access to multiple areas. If every area looks the same then this is easy too. A word of warning, don't try and control all of these areas yourself or you won't have time to focus on the things that only you can do. You'll burn out and you won't have time to live your life.

Allow the people you engage to manage these areas and to take on the responsibility. They will feel empowered and, guess what, they'll most likely do a better job.

Justine knew all about this type of concept from her corporate days as it is very similar to an Organisational Chart, but she was really struggling to see its relevance to her situation as a solo operator.

> "Andy, I get organisational charts. I've worked with them all my career, but it's just me. Do I really need to spend time on this one?"

> My question to Justine was "are there any parts of your business that you don't enjoy, any tasks that you're not good at?"

> "Sure there are. I don't love the accounting side. Actually, I don't enjoy admin in general. I could also do without trying to keep up with the tech side of things. It does my head in, stresses me out."

> "Ok, then there are the first two areas that you should be targeting to remove your name and add someone that is good at these areas."

"But it's still only me. Regardless of whether I like doing these tasks or not, I still have to do them."

"Yes, that may be true right now, but if you don't plan to remove yourself from these areas at some point you will continue to have a seven-day-a-week job that takes you away from your family. You are going to have to trust me on this one. Even if you remain the only person in your business, setting up this structure to flow through your business will bring many more benefits."

"Ok, I'm in. Let's do this. One thing though, can I call them Accountability Buckets? Because that's what I see them as, buckets of accountability."

"Sure you can. Actually, I like that one. I might start using it myself."

So, Justine was onboard. It was a bit of a struggle, but I knew there would be a time down the track that she would be thankful that she took time to implement this step.

I've also adopted the Accountability Buckets term, and smile to myself and think of our conversation every time I work through this part of the program with other business owners.

So from this point on, the areas of accountability will be referred to as **Accountability Buckets.** Thanks, Justine.

Some business owners make a conscious decision to not grow their business beyond them, not to build a team, and that's quite okay. Actually for many people that's a great strategy.

The one challenge in this situation is that we all have strengths and weaknesses, things we love to do and other things that we procrastinate on at best or, at worst, they don't get done at all.

There are also people just like Justine who think at the time it will only ever be them in the business. They later discover that they do in fact need to add team members (yes, this did happen to Justine as you'll find out in a future chapter).

If you've made the conscious decision to fly solo, you still need to set your business up so you can delegate or outsource tasks that you don't love and are not good at, whether on a regular basis or ad hoc when the need arises.

This is a big *mindset shift* for the majority of business owners, who think that it's more economical and profitable to do everything themselves. The mindset shift needed is that paying someone else to do the tasks that fall into your weakness and don't love to do categories is not an expense, it's an investment on which you will get a return.

Letting go is not easy for many people. It's a significant *mindset shift* and involves a high degree of trust. As a business owner, you have been conditioned to be responsible for everything, to know everything, to be the go-to person in the business. And that's understandable as it's probably your money, loan, house mortgage that have helped to fund and may continue to support the business.

No matter what stage you are at in your business right now, solo operator and wanting to stay that way, starting to build a team or with a team in place, taking time to plan and set up the foundation of your business will ensure:

- Everyone working in your business has a clearly defined role and knows what they are accountable for

- Business data can be easily entered, found and accessed and shared

- Projects and tasks are assigned to the relevant people and easily monitored, shared and updated

- You are able to secure data in certain areas and give access to relevant team members or external contractors

- Relevant communications are located in appropriate areas

- Your business will operate with consistency and efficiency, and time will be saved.

SUMMARY AND ACTIONS

The tools - I have created a free accountability map template that you can use. It can be found at the https://wfa.life/resources

The simple systems - The system is the accountability map. Think, if I had to delegate tasks in certain areas of my business, which would be the areas?

Implement this before you go any further. It can be adjusted (and probably will be) as you move forward, but make sure you get something in place now.

The mindset - The best person for the job is not always you. You may be the only one in your business right now and there may be things that only you can do, but this won't always be the case.

Actions to get to Step 1 - The Foundation

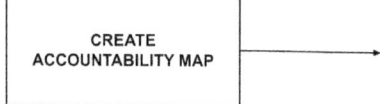

STOP!

Make TIME for LIFE.

Okay. I'm giving you permission to think about yourself.

Just you.

Guilt doesn't get a look in.

Your notes. Your LIFE.

Your chance to start living the Carpe Diem Way.

| My Carpe Diem Way

Write down what an ideal day would look like for YOU. Don't hold back.

"Don't count the days. Make the days count."

Muhammad Ali

ANDY'S STORY

How a change of time zone changed my life

It's only 4am but I'm wide awake, with a mix of jet lag and excitement. I really want to get stuck into work.

I set up my workspace, fire up the laptop, check my emails and make a Skype call. Kaycee assures me that everything is okay. Of course it is, I've only been gone a couple of days, just a little nervous about being so far away and in a different time zone.

I was still pretty set in my ways, keen to establish a daily schedule. We agreed to have a Skype call daily at 7.00am which was 3.00pm Australian time. Any other communications would be via email or Skype instant message.

Having established that the business hadn't gone under in the two days since I left, I then went about my work, and I remember thinking "this is absolutely no different", working on our events on my laptop from the other side of the world as opposed to working together in the office.

Maybe this working from anywhere could really succeed.

I worked for a little while longer before walking to the shops in the village. What a feeling it was, strolling alongside a fast-flowing river, looking up at the beautiful mountains, past houses hundreds of years old and then finding the local boulangerie.

Wow, baguettes, bread and more bread, croissants, and the pastries, OMG!

The variety of pastries on offer were not only extensive, the attention to detail and the obvious pride in presentation were amazing. Every one a delicate little work of art. My dad had spent his life as a pastry cook, specialising in French-style pastries, so I was familiar with some of what I

was seeing, and I couldn't help but think Dad would love this.

I settled on a baguette and a croissant for now. Surely it was too early for a chocolate éclair. Could I come back later? Mind you, the croissant didn't make it home. I devoured it moments into the 30-minute walk back to my apartment.

The sun was well and truly up over the mountains and I was still pinching myself as I walked beside the river, mesmerised by the colours and beauty of the snow-capped peaks that towered above me.

As scary as the thought of having to run my business from the other side of the world was, this felt right. I was excited and at peace at the same time.

Back to the office/apartment to do some more work. After all, I was meant to be working.

I moved my workspace to the table on the apartment deck. This was definitely the best office view I'd ever had. Yes, still pinching myself.

Lunchtime hit, and I couldn't resist any longer. It was time to put the bike gear on and head up into those magnificent mountains.

Not being one to ease into things, I decided to tackle a big one for my first ride, the climb made famous by the Tour de France, Alpe d'Huez.

Alpe d'Huez is famous for its 21 hairpin bends, all numbered and each dedicated to a TDF cyclist. The reason for the hairpin bends is it's the only way you could pave a way up to the top of a mountain this steep.

The top of the climb reaches an elevation of 1,852m. The total elevation gain is a significant 1,016m over a distance of just 11.8km. By comparison, our highest road in Australia finishes at Charlotte Pass at an elevation of 1,822m with the main climb having a total elevation gain of 924m over a distance of 27.3kms.

Adrenaline and my excitement had me pumping the pedals without stopping, pushing hard to get to the top in just over an hour.

I hooked my bike on the rack outside L'Indiana Cafe, discarded my helmet and gloves and found a table, joining the many other triumphant cyclists who had made it up the iconic mountain, swapping stories of our climbs, basking in the joy of accomplishment, the pain of the 21 bends all but forgotten.

I ordered my first French Alps 'café et pâtisserie', a short black and a perfect tarte au citron. I was hooked. That moment kicked off a coffee and cake (that's the Aussie version of café et pâtisserie) habit that continues to this day. It's a small guilt-free celebration of life.

The descent down the 21 hairpins was nothing short of an adrenaline rush, speeding back down into the amazing views of the valley far below.

A quick shower and freshen up and it was time for my first French lesson with Lionel.

I had decided prior to coming to France that I wanted to learn French, I had a very basic understanding but I wanted to learn more and staying for a longer period in the one place was the ideal opportunity.

Through a friend of a friend I managed to find someone that was willing to teach an Australian with a very little grasp on the French language French. Lionel, a teacher himself, was learning English in an English class run by the friend of a friend.

I'm not sure who was more nervous, the student or the teacher. I relaxed some when I realised Lionel's English was quite good, but unfortunately for Lionel the same couldn't be said for my French. Lionel came well prepared with worksheets that looked like they had come straight from the kindergarten syllabus, perfect for my level.

We ended the lesson agreeing to meet for une bière (one word that was easy to learn) at the local café-bar later so I could practice my French — now you're talking my language.

This was the start of a new rhythm in the days that followed, mixing work, cycling, coffee and cake, French lessons, making new friends and immersing myself in the village culture.

Working in a different time zone led me to understand that this new life wasn't just about where you work, it was also about when. I was fitting my work around my life and not the other way around as I had been doing for my entire working life.

I started to ask myself why I didn't work and live the same way at home. There was absolutely no reason why I shouldn't, but it took a change of time zone for me to realise that.

It was one of the many aha! moments served up on this trip.

| Step 2
Anywhere, Anytime, Any device

> *"Do not go where the path may lead, go instead where there is no path and leave a trail."*
>
> Ralph Waldo Emerson

Step 2 is where the magic happens, and happens fast. In the previous step I suggested that you would reap great benefits in the future from building a solid foundation. In this step, you reap the benefits and rewards straight away.

It's time to move your entire business to the Cloud. This includes your files and all the tools and technology you use to run your business.

This is a big step, actually a full stand-alone WFA program, and implementing it on its own will improve your operation exponentially.

Here's what will be covered to enable your business to run ***anywhere, at anytime, on any device:***

- What is the Cloud?
- The benefits of moving your entire business to the Cloud
- Choosing the cloud platform option that's right for you

- ACTION - Moving your entire business to the Cloud
- Pets make great friends, but terrible passwords
- ACTION - Implementing a Password Manager.

What is the Cloud?

First an explanation of what the Cloud is before I drill down into the reasons and benefits.

The three big questions I am constantly asked by business owners are: What is the Cloud? How does it work? Is it safe?

What is the Cloud? Well, it's not one of those white fluffy things that float around in the sky. Well, a cloud is, but the Cloud we're talking about isn't.

Your business data and the software you store and access from the Cloud are not drifting around in the wind. No, your business data, your personal data, your photos, your subscription software are all stored on a physical device at a physical location.

When you upload that file to "the Cloud", it gets saved to a hard drive not unlike the hard drive on your laptop. Okay, maybe a bit unlike it as it's a hard drive that is massively larger than you could possibly afford or store. This hard drive is located on a super powerful file server at various physical locations around the world called data centres.

Importantly, every time you upload a file it is not saved onto just one file server at one location. It is saved across multiple file servers at multiple locations. If something happens to one file server or data centre, your data is always safely backed up on another file server at another data centre, and always accessible without interruption.

That broadly answers the what is it and how it works, which leaves us with is it safe?

This I cover in more detail later in this chapter, and at this point all I'll say is that Google, Microsoft and all the other big cloud players spend hundreds of millions of dollars to secure your data, otherwise they wouldn't have a business.

More on this later.

The benefits of moving your entire business to the Cloud

There are many benefits to be had from moving your entire business into the Cloud. Here are my top four:

1. It secures your business against loss of data and business interruption

2. Gives you access to your business from *anywhere, at anytime on any device*

3. Saves you time and money

4. Collaboration is seamless and effective.

Moving your entire business to the Cloud is a game changer.

Life gets easier from this point forward like you would never have thought possible. You will be able to operate your business effectively from *anywhere, anytime, on any device.*

Benefit #1 - It secures your business against loss of data and business interruption

A question to ask yourself - What would happen if your laptop or server had a meltdown?

- Most of my business data, files and software would be lost

- Some data and software are backed up, but they would take a considerable time to recover

- Recovering the data would be a significant financial cost to the business

- The serious interruption to operations and sales would harm the business

- It would have very little impact on my business as all my data and software is stored in the Cloud.

The last item on this list is the aim of the game.

I'm sure you or one of your team have had a computer meltdown, a laptop stolen or maybe office equipment damaged by leaking water.

The thing is, you never know when disaster, at whatever level, may strike.

I live in the small coastal village of Tathra on the Far South Coast of NSW, Australia. In March 2018 Tathra was hit by a sudden, ferocious bushfire. The gale-force hot NW winds drove the fire rapidly through the dry, dense bush forest.

Within hours Tathra was under threat and all 1,600 residents were told to take anything important and evacuate immediately.

I packed my car and headed to the safety of my partner's place, 60kms away in Eden.

The fire devastated our small village. Sixty-nine houses were destroyed, 39 damaged and 30 caravans were lost.

It was four days before we were allowed back to see if our homes were still standing.

I was fortunate to return and find mine relatively unscathed, but the smell and sight of the damage to our coastal village was something I will never forget. I couldn't bring myself to leave home to see the destruction up close.

People lost their homes and irreplaceable possessions, and some also lost business records and precious memories that were stored on laptops and computers. These records and photos were unrecoverable, and a cruel blow on top of everything else.

2020 saw bushfires of an even greater scale destroy 5,900 buildings countrywide: houses, businesses and commercial sites.

Whatever the event or crisis, the result is inevitably the loss of precious data and interruption to business. At least having all your business data in the Cloud alleviates this problem. And don't worry, it's stored in more than one place

As Google states:

> **"We safeguard your data.**
> **Rather than storing each user's data on a single machine or set of machines, we distribute all data — including our own — across many computers in different locations."**

I had another real-life experience which made me aware of how important my decision to move my entire business into the Cloud was.

Here's what happened to me:

3rd June, 2014: Three days before boarding my flight to the French Alps for a two-month stay, my laptop had a meltdown — the dreaded 'black screen of death'. Dead, broken, completely unrecoverable.

Oh no. I was in the middle of organising a big event: 120 conference delegates traveling to Cape Town for 5-15 days in October. I couldn't afford ANY downtime at all.

3rd June, 2014: Once I settled down I fired up a spare laptop and was able to access every business file and software I use in the business without any interruption at all.

It was business as usual, because everything was in the Cloud. The meltdown of the laptop had zero effect on the running of my business.

6th June, 2014: Boarded my flight to France and spent the next two months running my business from the French Alps on my spare laptop.

I cycled, hiked, immersed myself in the village culture and worked on the big event, the Cape Town conference and extension tours.

10th August, 2014: Returned from an extremely successful two-month stint in the French Alps, bought a new laptop, turned it on and started working on it. No need to transfer files or software; it's all in the Cloud.

I can't imagine the stress, expense and other potential downsides I would've had to endure if I hadn't moved my entire business to the Cloud.

When I first started working with Justine, she was a little nervous about moving her entire business to the Cloud. She was concerned that her files might disappear if they weren't stored on her laptop. In her corporate life she had worked on a laptop, saving and working on files stored on the laptop hard drive, and also had access to the company server. The server was maintained by the IT department. She no longer had an IT department. Justine was IT (pun not intended).

> "But, Andy, I've been using Outlook, Word, Excel for my whole working career. They're all I know."

"When you work with your clients, do you ever advocate for, encourage or insist that to move forward they need to embrace change?"

"Of course. If you keep doing the things you've always done, nothing will change, and you can't possibly move forward."

"So, are the current tools you're using in your business working for you?"

"Not really, everything takes so much time. It's clunky, and without my laptop I can't access information when I'm out and about. I had a client meeting the other day and the information I needed to discuss was on a thumb drive I had left at home. So embarrassing."

"We can resolve all of this by moving your business to the Cloud."

Justine decided to take the leap, and we worked towards moving her entire business to the Cloud, a decision that would soon bring a reward that she hadn't considered.

About six weeks later, Justine let me know she was excited but nervous about buying a new laptop.

"Andy, I'm really excited about updating my laptop. I can get a really good deal, but I'm dreading having to transfer all my data and programs across from one laptop to another. I've never had to worry about this, the guys in IT departments always took care of this stuff. I'm absolutely dreading it. It's stressing me out."

"Well, I've got good news for you. There is nothing to transfer. You've moved everything to the Cloud, so it doesn't matter what device you're on. All you need to do is fire up the laptop, install Google Chrome, log in to your Google Workspace account and you're good to go."

"You're kidding, what about all the software?"

"It's all in the Cloud. There is nothing to transfer or install."

Justine's new laptop, a Mac, arrived. She started it up, went through the startup wizard for the laptop, signed into her Google Workspace account and she was all good to go. I didn't need to help her in any way.

"Andy, I can't believe how easy that was. I don't know why I was stressing."

Benefit #2 - Gives you access to your business from anywhere, at anytime on any device.

So, if securing your business against loss of data and business interruption is the #1 reason for moving to the Cloud, the next important reason is that you will have access to your business from *anywhere, at anytime, and on any device.*

Which means you will be able to take control of where you work, when you work and what device you work on.

Let me explain the key difference in how the Cloud works and how we have traditionally worked on and managed our digital business data.

Before the Cloud came along, files were saved to a particular device, individual computer hard drives, external storage devices, thumb drives or the company server.

Whichever method was used, to access the file you needed the physical device it was stored on. If the file was on a device in the office you were unable to access it from elsewhere.

If you needed to work on files at home, you would save them onto a thumb drive, work on the files at home and hope you remembered to update them back at the office the next day.

This way of tracking versions often gets quite confusing. Changes get overwritten accidentally, the wrong version gets picked and shared, causing further confusion and frustration, file names become unmanageable and different people rename the file differently. It often takes several phone calls and emails just to work out IF you're working on the right version.

The same goes with emails and calendars. Emails you receive on one device don't show up on the other, and changing a date in a calendar event on one device doesn't synchronise with your other devices.

You miss responding to emails, don't have access to the email you need information from, miss meetings, and get time zones wrong for meetings with your team, clients or potential clients.

Next came the option to synchronise your data between devices. This was a big step forward, but it was a manual process and, done incorrectly, resulted in the overwriting of current important data.

This does not happen when using the Cloud. The Cloud works differently as there is only one version of any file or data in one place that is viewable and editable from many places or devices. No matter where or what device you are accessing and updating the information from, you are only ever looking at and working on one file, *one version of the truth,* and this can be accessed from **anywhere, at anytime, on any device.**

What if I don't have an internet connection?

This is another question I'm asked all the time. Think about it though, how often are we really without an internet connection these days? It is much more likely the old file server that you forgot to back up has a meltdown and you lose all your data at once, or you lose days or weeks trying to recover the data.

The Cloud, in particular Google Drive, offers the option to make sure

some or even all (not recommended but possible) of your data is available offline and you have complete control over this.

If you really must work while you're on that flight instead of kicking back and reading a book or watching a movie, then you can. If you really need to access the net while you're on a cruise, you can. It's just super expensive. If you're hiking or on some other adventure, you may not have internet access for a day or two or even longer, depending on where you are... so plan for that.

Really though, the better option is to just enjoy the hike or whatever offline activity you are on, to be present and seize the day. The work will still be there when you get back.

If you do decide to work offline, there is no need to worry about losing all the work you've done. As soon as you get your internet connection back, all the files you were working on are automatically synchronised and backed up into the cloud to access from *anywhere, at anytime and on any device.*

Let's have a deeper look at the benefits of the any device part of this statement:

The only way you can access the files and software stored on your local hard drive on your laptop or your server is by having access to that particular physical device. If you're operating in the Cloud, you're able to access the data and software stored in it from any device that has a web browser, and most of the cloud resources now also have an app to make it even easier on mobile devices.

I can access every, yes every, file in my business on my mobile phone. I could even access all my files on your mobile phone if you let me.

Allow me to share a real-life experience where I benefited greatly from

being able to access all of my business from my mobile phone:

> I was meeting my accountant to sign off on my business and personal tax returns.
>
> There were a few items that the accountant needed some more information on before everything could be signed off though, one of which was a breakdown of the original purchase price and tax details of a property I had sold in the current tax year. The property had been purchased 10 years before.
>
> The accountant needed a copy of the sales contract, which contained the relevant information.
>
> Normally this would mean my going away to search the paper archives for the contract, and then scanning and forwarding it to the accountant, and making another appointment to complete.
>
> Instead, I picked up my phone, opened up Google Drive and put in the search terms for the contract. I was able to locate it within seconds and share the document there and then.
>
> I can still see the look on my accountant's face, the look of disbelief that I was able to find and share a 10-year-old document within minutes from my mobile phone.
>
> I had saved myself and my accountant time, and I had also saved myself the expense of an additional appointment.

Have you ever left home without your phone, unlikely as that is these days, or your laptop and really needed to access some business files while you were out and about? Just find a computer, a library, a friend, and if it's in the Cloud you will be able to access whatever you need.

I could've found the same property contract I needed using the accountant's

computer if I hadn't had my phone with me (unlikely).

The Cloud is your ticket to freedom. You can access your business from **anywhere, at anytime, on any device,** so you can spend more time living life outside of your business.

Benefit #3 - Saves you time and money

The Cloud will *save you time and money.*

You will no longer need to invest in powerful and expensive file servers or laptops. The Cloud is your server, and all your data is in the Cloud so you no longer need massive storage space on your local machines or laptops. You can get away with purchasing lower-priced laptops with minimal storage.

You can also do away with all those expensive backup devices as everything will be securely backed up in the Cloud instead.

Once you move to monthly subscription-based software, updates are included and, better still, happen in the background. You can usually lock in the subscription rate, saving yourself some money too.

You no longer need to spend massive chunks of money on desktop software for each of your laptops or computers, nor purchase or install those annoying and expensive annual or more frequent updates.

The software you buy now costs less and you get more. The prices of Microsoft Office back in 2007: Office Professional $499; Office Small Business $449; Office Standard $399.

The comparable product at time of writing is around $210.00/user for either MS365 Business or Google Workspace Business.

You no longer need to stay back at night getting the backup started. Your

data are automatically and constantly backed up in the Cloud.

Nor is there any need to spend time installing updates manually on the server and every machine or having one of your team doing it. All your software is automatically updated regularly in the Cloud, and when you access the software you are always using the latest version no matter which device you are on.

In a worst-case scenario, you simply need to hit an 'update now' button when prompted from time to time.

Collaborating on documents in the Cloud rather than emailing updated versions back and forth via email also saves everyone a huge amount of time, and the time you've spent accessing and working on your business when you're off-site is time you won't need to spend back in the office.

The Cloud *saves you time and money.*

Benefit #4 - Collaboration is seamless and effective

The next big benefit of using cloud technology is that *collaboration is seamless and effective.*

Trust me, collaborating in the Cloud will supercharge your productivity.

You'll find yourself eliminating time-wasting duplication, increasing the opportunities for real-time brainstorming, streamlining the scheduling process, and minimising the confusion and errors that typically arise when there is no common platform to work from. And it all gets done with efficiency from *anywhere, at anytime and on any device.*

The two particular areas where collaboration is most seamless and effective involve calendars and documents. Google stands out here, so I'm going to use Google Calendar and Google Docs to explain how it works.

Let's start with calendars:

We've all used calendars to keep track of appointments, events and even projects, and we've all had our own personal preferences when it comes to format: wall calendars, desk calendars, personal notebook calendars, a paper diary...

The team calendar was on the wall for all to see. This may or may not have included when staff were away on holiday, but there was a separate leave calendar that only the boss could see. Individual team members also had their own personal diaries to track their own schedule that they carried with them, and they may have also had a desk calendar. These were just the work schedules; then there was the calendar on the fridge at home for family life.

There were a couple of major problems with this system, the first of which was that no calendar could ever be in more than one place at a time. You can't view your office calendar while discussing a project with a client. You can't see your home calendar to check there are no personal clashes with business events you are rsvping.

The second problem was you were unable to effectively collaborate in and outside your organisation. Their availability was mostly only known to individual team members, unless they duplicated their personal schedule on the team calendar, when of course they needed to remember to amend both calendars as things happened.

The end result was often double and triple bookings when you were unable to commit to an event until you got back to the office to check the team calendar, so important meetings were missed, and the family was not happy when you had a business meeting at the same time as the school awards.

It was chaos.

Electronic calendars came along as technology progressed, though the early versions only resolved some of these problems. The first electronic calendars didn't allow for collaboration. You could only access your own calendar from your laptop or device.

Google calendar resolves all of the above and calms the chaos.

Google calendar is in the Cloud — you guessed it — so there is only *one version of the truth* and you can access this version from *anywhere, at anytime and on any device.*

Google calendar allows you to share your calendar, create collaborative team calendars, view multiple calendars at one time, and invite people to events. And when integrated with a third-party tool like Calendly, it enables people outside your organisation to check your availability and book an appointment with you.

Locking in appointments with clients was hard work for Justine.

> "Andy, making appointments with my clients is a nightmare: so much back and forth with emails, sms and phone calls to try and find a time that works for both of us. Then something comes up and they want to change the date and we have to do it all again. It takes up so much of my time."

> "I have a solution for that one, Justine. What if you could send a link to your client that shows your availability? They could then pick a time that suits them and click on a button to confirm. They get a confirmation email and can add it to their own calendar, and it automatically goes into your calendar without you doing a thing."

> "That would be amazing, but is it really possible? I don't actually want

them to see all my appointments with other clients."

"That's okay. They won't see any of your appointments, only the times you are available."

"I'm in, but it sounds complicated."

"It's much simpler than you think. All you need is a tool called Calendly, which you can link to your Google Calendar. You create some event types like 30 minutes meeting, 45 minutes meeting, etc., and then send the link to the client."

"Wow, I'm definitely in."

It didn't take long to implement Calendly for Justine. She started with the free version, but soon upgraded to the premium when she discovered the USD8/month was well and truly worth it.

"Andy, Calendly is amazing. It's not just saving me time and stress, but I'm finding my appointment conversion rate has doubled. It's so much easier for potential clients to book an appointment now, so I'm getting more bookings and more business as a result."

So when you work with Google calendar **collaboration is seamless and effective,** especially when you integrate it with another tool such as Calendly.

Calendars done. Next up are documents:

Before the Cloud came along, when working with documents we would use versions that were updated and renamed after major updates or collaboration. These versions were 'saved as' on individual devices or a server, renamed by collaborators and then sent back as an attachment on an email or even shared on a thumb drive.

When working in the Cloud, multiple people can access and work with the data at the same time without needing to create new versions, since there is only ever **one version of the truth**. In fact this book was written, edited and proofread by collaborating on a Google Doc in the Cloud.

I'll use Google Docs to explain:

When I say Google Docs, this includes all of the Google Docs family: Docs (word processing), Sheets (spreadsheets) and Slides (presentations). Google Docs has many great features that power collaboration — and here are two of the best — Google docs enables you to:

- Control the permissions individual collaborators have on each document
- Collaborate on a document in real time or each collaborator's own time.

When you share a Google document with collaborators, you can *control the permissions individual collaborators have on each document,* and choose to give them access to edit or comment only.

Edit - This allows collaborators to directly edit your document, to add, change or delete text.

Comment only - Collaborators are only able to comment on areas of the document. They can highlight relevant parts of the document and add a comment for document owner action. This means you have total control of the content, are the only one who can edit the document, and that your work will not, intentionally or unintentionally, be changed.

The bottom line is you have complete control over your document at all times, and can give, amend or revoke these permissions at any time.

Let me answer a pertinent question, outside of collaboration — one that

is always asked, especially by people transitioning from using Microsoft Word, Excel, etc. What happens if you want to share a document with someone who does not have a Google account?

Not a problem. You can always share as a 'view only' document. You can create a link that can be used to open the document from any device without the need for any software at all.

Same again here: you have complete control over your document at all times and you can give, amend or revoke these permissions at any time.

Now here's where real power and productivity come in: you can **collaborate on a document in real time or each collaborator's own time.**

Collaborators can work on the document in their **own time,** at a time that works for their work schedule.

Collaborating in **real time** provides the opportunity to brainstorm as you go, so the end result is potentially much better and always much quicker.

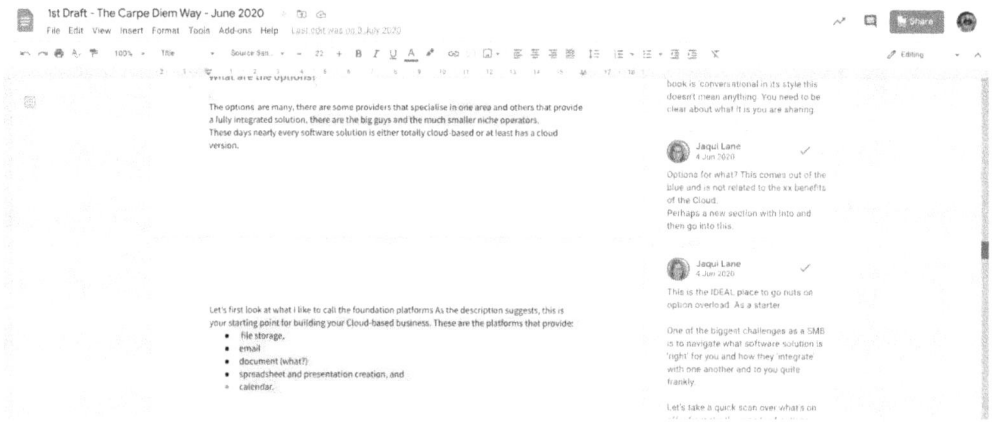

In the above is an example, I am collaborating with my book coach, Jaqui Lane, on this book. Jaqui, poor Jaqui, gave feedback and advice, like lots of

feedback on various sections, by simply highlighting the area and adding a comment.

The comment shows on the right-hand side of the page without altering the actual document content. I can choose whether to take the advice or not, change the document and then tick the comment to resolve it so it disappears.

And that, folks, is how working in the Cloud **collaboration is seamless and effective.**

You can access step-by-step tutorials on how to share, control permissions and collaborate on Google Docs at https://wfa.life/resources

Choosing the Cloud platform option that's right for you

One of the biggest challenges as a business owner is to navigate what software solutions are right for you and how they integrate with one another.

You now know the benefits of moving your entire business into the Cloud, and you understand some of the strategies you can put in place to work effectively from *anywhere, at anytime, on any device.*

There is more than one cloud platform to choose from though, so which do you pick?

Working out what each of them does, how they connect (or not), how much you have to pay, who can advise you on what options you need and how to build it, let alone how to maintain it, is a nightmare.

For many people, it all gets too hard, and it's easier to keep using what you've always used even if it's not really working. It's just easier to avoid the pain of change.

My number one tip here is that less is better. Use a platform that includes an integrated suite of tools that work together and also integrate seamlessly with third party tools.

Beware of the next shiny object —the new tech tool that promises to be your productivity silver bullet.

This is where I come in. Testing the next best thing is part of what I do. I've spent thousands of hours and thousands of dollars testing, learning how to use, discarding and finding the next tool, to end up with a small suite of tools that work effectively.

The end result of this ongoing research is that I use and share one integrated cloud platform with an integrated suite of tools in it and a handful of outside tools that integrate seamlessly.

Google Workspace from Google is my platform of choice after many years of testing, trialling, and discovering what works best for me and the businesses I work with. I don't receive any form of revenue from Google, I just believe in their products.

The strategies in this book use the Google Workspace platform and its integrated suite of tools along with a handful of third-party tools that also integrate, all of which I will introduce you to as we work through the five steps.

For the purposes of this chapter and this step, you need to decide on your main cloud-based storage and integrated tools platform. This is the platform that will set you up to work from **anywhere, at anytime, on any device,** and you may very well already be using one.

Your integrated platform should include these tools as a minimum:

- Online file storage

- Email

- Calendar

- Tools to create documents, spreadsheets, presentations

- Text and video chat

- Video meeting options.

These are the major players in this field:

Google - Google's business offering is Google Workspace, a suite of tools that integrate and work together. Google Drive for online file storage, Gmail for email, Google Calendar, Google Docs (word documents), Sheets (spreadsheets) and Slides (presentations), Keep for notes, Google Photos (great for business and your personal life), Google Chat for short text message chats, YouTube for videos, Google Meet for video meetings, Google maps and plenty more.

Microsoft - MS365 is Microsoft's main business offering, they also have a kit of tools that work together: OneDrive for online file storage, Outlook for email, calendar, MS Office tools Word, Excel and Powerpoint, OneNote for notes, Skype for chat and videos.

Apple - iWorks is Apple's suite offering: ICloud for online file storage, Apple Mail for email, calendar, Pages (word documents), Numbers (spreadsheets), Keynote (presentations), calendar, iMovie for video editing and Notes for notes.

Dropbox - Dropbox is a powerful solution for online file storage, and that's all it does. Dropbox doesn't have its own suite of tools, but it does integrate with external tools.

So, which one of these is right for your business? It may depend on what

tools you already have in place, and what you and your team are most comfortable working with. Then again, staying doing things the way you've always done them may not be such a good idea either.

I've used many of these solutions at various points in my business life — some more than others, some a good experience, others not so.

It all started with Microsoft for me, as I'm sure it did and still does for many others. This was back in the day when there were only Word, Excel and PowerPoint. Microsoft had the market.

Just as the Commonwealth Bank gave themselves an advantage by introducing banking to school kids in their early school years through their Dollarmites program, Microsoft cornered the business software market in the early days. Microsoft Office tools were the only option for many people.

In both of these scenarios, they conditioned people to use their products from early on, to the point that it was much easier to stay with them than change when competitors came along.

Competitors did eventually come along: Apple, Google, Dropbox, Box to name a few.

Online storage space soon became crowded, but Microsoft not only had the jump on their competitors in online storage space, they also benefited hugely from being years ahead with word processing, spreadsheets and presentation software.

In the early days, Google Docs was not a patch on Microsoft Word. Google was playing catch-up big time. People had been using Outlook as their email for many years. You may still be using it and quietly saying to yourself as you read this I'll never move across to Google.

Google was traditionally more consumer-focused until the release of Google Apps for Work, their challenge to Microsoft in the business space. Google continued to refine and improve their business offering, in 2016 rebranded to G-Suite, and then in late 2020 to the current (at time of writing) Google Workspace. Previously a long way behind in the market share race, they have made significant progress in both the small business and large organisation spaces.

I decided to take the leap away from the Microsoft camp and into the Google camp some years ago and have never looked back. The ease of use, superior collaboration experience, advantage of many tools that work seamlessly together and, most of all, the best search engine in the world, work equally throughout the entire suite of tools.

So back to the question which is the best platform for you?

While I'll recommend Google Workspace every day of the week, if you're currently using Microsoft 365 and it's working for you, stick with it. If you're not set up in the Cloud at all, then I would recommend Google Workspace, it's cost-effective, user-friendly and super for collaboration.

If you're using a mix, Microsoft for email, some files in OneDrive, some in Dropbox, some on various laptops and/or the server, then now is the time for a plan to put everything into one place. Again, I believe that Google Workspace is the way to go.

Find the option that works for you and use it exclusively. This is one case where it is okay to put all your eggs in one basket. Why? Because it means you only ever need to look in one basket for most of what you need to run your business.

Once you have chosen a provider, you need to commit to having everything in the Cloud. Not some, not most, EVERYTHING.

This will ensure your entire business is accessible from anywhere, at anytime, on any device.

ACTION - Moving your entire business to the Cloud

The very first step you need to take is to choose and sign up for your preferred integrated cloud platform. You will find links to the options on the resources page https://wfa.life/resources

Then comes the big move. It's time to gather up ALL your business files from various locations and move them into one place. That one place for the businesses I work with is Google Drive, the cloud storage area of Google Workspace.

It can be a relatively big project, especially if you have files scattered between laptops, external drives, thumb drives, several cloud storage systems and maybe a server.

This is a project worth doing though, because moving all of your files into one place in the Cloud will tick all the boxes:

- It secures your business against loss of data and business interruption
- Gives you access to your business from anywhere, at anytime on any device
- Saves you time and money
- Makes collaboration seamless and effective.

This is a task that can be done over time. Actually, it's best done in stages over a period of time.

It needs to be done methodically, and here's where the foundation you built in step 1 comes in. It's time to use the second row of your accountability map to organise your files as you go.

Business name - Accountability Map

			BUSINESS OWNER WHO?			
OPERATIONS WHO?	SALES WHO?	MARKETING WHO?	TECHNOLOGY WHO?	MANAGEMENT WHO?	FINANCE WHO?	HUMAN RESOURCES WHO?

File Storage Structure

OPERATIONS	SALES	MARKETING	TECHNOLOGY	MANAGEMENT	FINANCE	HUMAN RESOURCES

This is where the consistency starts. Moving all your files into your cloud storage platform is a great opportunity to have a big cull and sort out. It's an opportunity to declutter and get organised.

The first thing you need to do before you start moving any files is to create top level folders or shared drives in Google Drive based on your accountability map. Keep it simple. If you're using Google Drive, Google has the best search engine in the world, so there is no need to create a rabbit warren of folders, sub-folders, sub-sub-folders etc. Resist at all costs.

Google Workspace allows you to move files using a feature called

Filestream. It's awesome, and much easier and more productive.

Try to delete files you no longer need, and reduce the clutter. If you really must keep files you haven't used for a long time but think you may need in the future, create a folder called Archive and store them there, away from your working folders.

This is an important step. Keep going until you have moved EVERYTHING, and try not to leave duplicates at the original destination. Cut and paste rather than copy and paste.

If you feel uncomfortable or concerned about losing files, copy them to Google Drive, then go back and delete from the original destination once you are confident that you have everything safely stored in your cloud platform.

That's it. Keep chipping away and over time you will end up with all your files safely secured in the Cloud and accessible from anywhere, at anytime and on any device.

Here is another real-life example and compelling reason why moving your entire business to the Cloud makes sense:

In 2020 the COVID-19 pandemic hit. In a matter of weeks the whole world was going into various levels of lockdown, businesses were having to shut their doors and those that could still operate had set up their teams to work from home.

Schools also closed, so parents not only had to adjust to working from home, but overnight they also became homeschooling teachers. There was little time for preparation. It just had to happen. One of my clients was thankful for the position they found themselves in to get through this dilemma:

Jen manages a softwood timber harvesting business with a team of 30, most of whom are out in the field.

The field team were able to continue working, but Jen now needed to be home with her young son, and work from home like the other office staff.

Fortunately, Jen had moved most of their files to the Cloud while on the WFA Program.

> "If this had happened 12 months ago, it would have been near impossible to keep the business running. We could've done it, but it would have meant so many extra hours.
>
> "We could have accessed the server from outside the office, but it was so slow. I'm so glad we moved everything to the Cloud, now working from home is practically no different from working in the office.
>
> "The only difference is I get interruptions from my son instead of the office chat. That's okay though. It's actually been really special having more time with him."

You should now be set up to manage this same situation.

Pets make great friends, but terrible passwords

Okay, who uses their pet's name as their password? Who's been here… 'Someone figured out my password, and now I have to rename my dog?'

It's best to keep your pet as a friend, not as the source of your passwords. Because this is the truth:

> **81% of hacking-related breaches leveraged either stolen and/or weak passwords.**

One of the biggest concerns people have with the Cloud is they have heard

that it's not safe. They hear stories from business colleagues about getting hacked.

The grapevine tells them the Cloud is not secure.

Google, Microsoft, Amazon, all the cloud solution providers, spend hundreds of millions of dollars on securing their customers' data and it's one of the reasons most large banks, financial institutions and companies are migrating all their data and operations to the Cloud.

They are not only protecting their customer data, they're protecting their current and future business. They wouldn't have a business if they didn't secure their customers' data.

The biggest vulnerability in any organisation is always the end user, the people who use the same passwords or variance of passwords for every login in their life, both personal and business.

This doesn't just apply to the Cloud, it also applies to the entire digital world we live in. We need a login and password for everything we do: digital is the gateway to our business and personal data.

According to the Verizon 2017 Data Breach Investigations Report, over 70% of employees reuse passwords at work.

Other alarming statistics from the same report reveal:

Individual users reusing passwords at home translate to their work environment.

Even though 91% of people know reusing passwords is poor practice, 59% reuse their passwords everywhere – at home and at work.

I know many people who use the word 'password' as their password, and others who use 1234 or their birth date or that of a loved one.

Why then do

87% admit they frequently reuse passwords despite knowing better?

Imagine if the wrong person gets hold of the password you use everywhere, that password you use because it makes your life easier. That one password is all that is needed by that wrong person to get access to most of your digital world, both personal and business.

Because everyone is too busy, they don't have time, they have too many passwords, it's much easier and more time efficient to use the same one, and they don't know of a better option.

Well, there is a much better option, an option that will not only store your passwords securely in one place, but also generate secure passwords. You will no longer need to think of or remember a password again. It's called a *password manager.*

And you can add an additional layer of security on top of that: two-step authentication.

If you have a business, or even if you don't, and you don't use a password manager in your business and personal life, then you are leaving yourself and your business open to data breaches, fraud, employee theft, and hackers gaining access to your sensitive business data. The cost to your business is potentially catastrophic.

What are the options and how does a password manager work?

There are a number of options to choose from, and here are some of the key players as at time of writing:

- LastPass
- Dashlane

- Roboform
- 1Password
- Sticky Password
- Keepass.

As with all things technology though, nothing stays the same for very long. New options are created every day and the current alternatives are constantly being updated and improved.

I've used two of the above. I started out on Roboform before moving to LastPass, my password manager of choice and the one I recommend.

In simple terms, a password manager stores all your passwords in a secure vault and you access them with a single master password. You can access your vault of passwords on any device.

A password manager also allows you to generate secure passwords: a jumble of characters that have no meaning, the number of which you get to choose. These generated passwords are automatically stored in your password manager vault.

You only need to remember one password, which can and should be long, with a mix of characters, numbers, and upper and lowercase.

Using a passphrase is a great way to create a long, non-dictionary-based, difficult-to-crack master password that you can easily remember.

A passphrase is a sequence of words strung together in a nonsensical sentence. These are usually words that mean something to you, but not to anyone else. You pick a number of completely unrelated words and put them together to create your secure password. You should change some character types.

V0lk$wagenSummerYellow!Tulip

This method results in a password that is secure, but easy for you to remember as you are using words that have meaning to you.

You may need to write your master password down to start with, keep it on a piece of paper just for a short while, but as you'll be using it continually it won't take too long before you remember it and can destroy that piece of paper (just like in Mission Impossible).

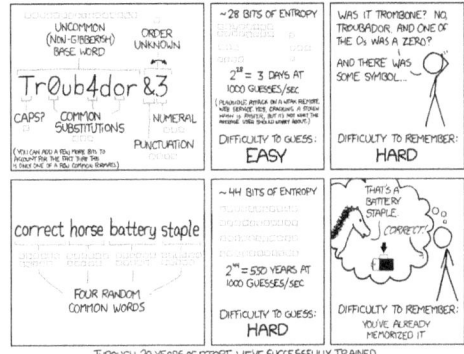

LastPass is my password manager of choice. They state on their website:

> **"LastPass encrypts your Vault before it goes to the server using 256-bit AES encryption. Since the Vault is already encrypted before it leaves your computer and reaches the LastPass server, not even LastPass employees can see your sensitive data!"**

To break that statement down into something we can all relate to, 256-bit AES encryption has been used by the US Government to protect classified information since June 2003.

Without going into too many technical details, LastPass uses a process whereby an encryption key is created locally and never leaves your machine. This key is used to decrypt your Vault (passwords) once it comes back.

LastPass does not have access to your master password or your password vault contents, and there is a method for recovering your LastPass vault without LastPass knowing your master password.

The most important feature of LastPass is its ability to generate a secure password for you — a jumble of characters, 10, 20, 30 right up to 99 characters long. The more characters, the harder it is to crack. The beauty of it is though, you don't need to remember these passwords, they are safely stored in your password vault, and all you need is your master password to access them.

A reminder: pets make great friends but terrible passwords!

I actually don't know any of my passwords. I don't need to know them! They are all generated jumbles of characters stored in LastPass.

You can also store other sensitive data in LastPass, such as passport information, licences, bank details, credit card information, health care

card details. You can have everything you will ever need access to securely stored and available from anywhere, even your mobile phone or iPad.

Need your passport information when you're out and about? No problem, it's on your phone. Can't remember the bank pin number you just changed? No problem, it's in your LastPass vault, which you can access from anywhere, at anytime and on any device.

Two-step authentication - security on top of security

The next level of security that should be used EVERYWHERE possible in your digital world is two-step authentication. You may already be familiar with this without even knowing it as it's the method most banks have been using for some time.

Two-step authentication involves using a password and a second step where you need to enter a time-sensitive numeric code provided from an external source. This code can be sent as an SMS message or generated in a two-step authenticator app. It is generally only valid for a short period of time, usually around 30 seconds, before it refreshes to a new code.

Let me recommend upfront here, while receiving a SMS message may sound like the easiest option, and it may be most of the time, it falls down when you're working from another country. When overseas you probably use a local SIM (my recommendation) or it costs you a fortune to receive SMS messages.

The best option to cover all bases is using an Authenticator App. My app of choice is Google Authenticator, which works well and is part of the Google ecosystem central to my digital world. It really is easy to use and it's free. You download the app to your mobile phone and then work through a simple setup wizard for each app or platform you wish to secure. You only need to do this once.

You can then view and input the relevant six-digit numeric code from your app into the site you're logging into and you're all safe and secure.

Accounting software Xero for instance not only allows two-step authentication, it is mandatory.

2SA is optional for most users, but it's mandatory for all users of an Australian Xero product, except users of My Payroll. This is to support the ATO's requirements for digital service providers. Xero products include Xero Business edition, Xero HQ, My Xero Partner Edition, Practice Manager, Workpapers and WorkflowMax.

You need to check for a two-step authentication option on all the sites you use, and activate it on every one possible, including your password manager. Especially your password manager. Give yourself peace of mind. Go on, do it — it's worth the effort.

ACTION - Implementing a password manager action steps

1. Sign up for a password manager for yourself and your team

2. Everyone needs their own password manager. Password manager user logins should never be shared

3. Save all of your current passwords to the password manager

4. Change each of your passwords by generating a secure password for each login using the password manager

5. Implement two-step authentication for as many logins as possible

6. Secure other sensitive business information, bank accounts, credit cards, registrations by saving into your password manager

7. Get all your team members to do the same.

That's it. You've moved your business to the Cloud, and you can now access it from anywhere, at anytime and on any device. You can find that file, look up that information, even send out that invoice no matter where you are. You can do it from your phone as you enjoy a latte at the local coffee shop.

You're now sleeping easy knowing that your business data is safe and secure, and you no longer need to think of new passwords. And you are able to log in to all of your sites and software easily from anywhere, at anytime and on any device.

You're already feeling like you don't need to be AT work ALL the time, and this is just the beginning. Read on to unlock even more time for life.

SUMMARY AND ACTIONS

The tools - Integrated cloud technology platform of choice (my preference is Google Workspace), Password Manager

The simple systems - Use your Accountability Map to organise your online storage, and share and collaborate on documents and calendars. Always generate secure passwords using a Password Manager.

The mindset - The Cloud is safe. The biggest vulnerability is the end user. There is no need to have multiple versions of a document; it's okay to only have one version of the truth.

Actions to get to Step 2 - Anywhere, Any Time, Any Device

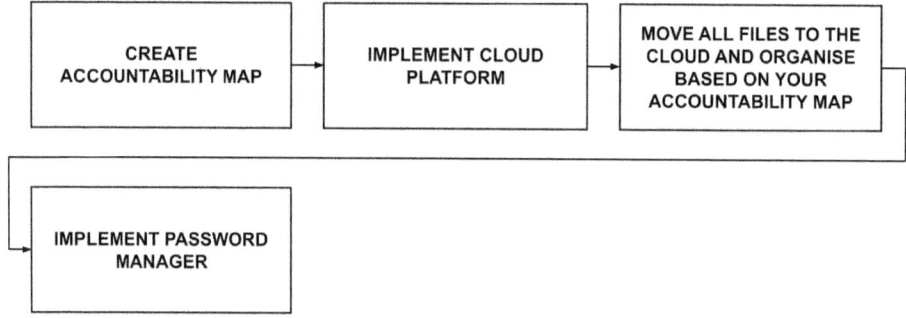

STOP!

Make TIME for LIFE.

Is your WHY starting to become clear?

Why should you start making TIME for LIFE?

So what's getting in your way?

While you've been reading this book, how many times have you said I can't do that because xyzxyz (insert your excuse).

It's your life. Your notes. Your WHY.

Your chance to start living the Carpe Diem Way.

| My Carpe Diem Way

What's getting in your way?

List the three excuses that keep coming up.

_____
_____
_____
_____
_____
_____
_____
_____
_____
_____
_____
_____

"Only put off until tomorrow what you are willing to die having left undone."

Pablo Picasso

ANDY'S STORY

Same same, but different

The biggest impact on my life during my stay in the French Alps was breaking free of the conditioning of when to work.

After a couple of weeks I became more flexible. If the weather was overcast in the morning I'd keep working and finish a bit later. If it was a nice day I'd head out for an early ride and skip the morning work session. I didn't necessarily do eight hours' work — some days much less, some days a little more, some days none at all.

I returned from my WFA French Alps experiment a changed man. My conference business had not only survived this experiment, it had actually thrived. The business was working more productively as a result of the systems we had put in place. Kaycee was feeling more empowered than ever, the big event we had been working on while I was in France was only a couple of months away and all was looking good.

I brought my newly discovered work practices back to Australia, and working in 8-10 hour blocks was a thing of the past. Instead I continued to mix work with activity, working for shorter times and stepping away for regular breaks.

There were no huge mountains or French cafés, but I had a beautiful beach to walk on, some nice coastal rides I could enjoy and few good waves around to catch on my SUP when the conditions were right.

It didn't matter that I was back in the same time zone again, because my mindset had changed.

There were more changes on the way. Kaycee had made the decision

to move to Melbourne with her partner the following year. That wasn't a problem though. We'd set up the business so anyone could work from anywhere, not just me. All she needed was a laptop and she was all set to continue her great work.

Under normal circumstances I would be up for hiring a new staff member, finding the right person, training them, hoping I had picked well — all very time-consuming, not to mention costly.

Now this didn't need to happen. Kaycee moved to Melbourne, had a few days to settle in and then it was business as usual.

We had a big event on the books for later that year, one of the biggest events we had ever put together. A five-day conference in Cape Town for 120 delegates, including options for pre-conference extensions to the Game Parks, and a post-conference Victoria Falls and Okavango Delta package.

It was a really big deal, over 12 months in the planning, six of those months with Kaycee working from Melbourne and me from Tathra, and for two of those months Kaycee worked from Melbourne and I worked from the French Alps.

Now both Kaycee and myself were benefiting from the changes we had put in place.

Same same, but different!

| Step 3
Getting the processes out of your head

> "Organise around business functions, not people. Build systems within each business function. Let systems run the business and people run the systems. People come and go but the systems remain constant."
>
> Michael Gerber, E-Myth Revisited

Creating and documenting systems for a business are not at the top of many owners' to-do list. They're too busy making sales, managing the team, locking in customer meetings and getting whatever job needs to be done, done.

They haven't got time to create systems. They're busy as it is. It would be great to be able to delegate some of this busyness, but many of the tasks are too hard to explain. It's easier to just do it themselves.

Yes, maybe it is easier to just do it yourself, but the problem is you'll need to keep doing it yourself, every day, every week, month, year and decade. And when you're not there it won't get done, because no one else knows how to do it.

You're stuck in the I'm indispensable trap, and it's of your own making OR desire. Maybe you like it, that feeling of being needed — being the 'go-to'

person. Chances are you're probably too tired to really think about it, but occasionally, or perhaps more and more, you're starting to wonder how you can become less indispensable but not less across what's going on.

It's a tough place, the transition from being there in your business all the time to creating a business that is there for you, that you can work in but not on EVERY DAY. And it's this mindset barrier that drives the 'I'm not convinced that it's worth the effort' response.

In this chapter I introduce you to a simple workflow and a task and project management platform to use to work through Steps 3,4 & 5.

The simple workflow is the *WFA Systems Build & Action Flow*.

I've developed the workflow over many years of testing and refining. It has been successfully implemented by the business owners I work with as well as in my own business.

The task and project management platform is *Asana*.

> "Bring your teams, work, and apps together from anywhere in one tool with Asana. Get started to plan and manage all your team's work, from start to end." - Asana website

This is what Asana states on their website and I agree, it really does allow you to plan and manage all your team's work from start to finish. Just like it manages the *WFA Systems Build & Action Flow* from start to finish.

There are other similar tools and platforms, and I've tried many of them. After years of trials and tests, Asana is the platform that came up trumps for me and the one that is used to manage the *WFA Systems Build & Action Flow*.

Asana has free and paid versions. The free version allows for up to 15 team

members and may possibly be all most businesses need, especially to get started.

I encourage you to embrace **Asana.** It will become a core asset in your business.

Justine was ready to make that tough transition. Her leadership coaching business was starting to operate with much more efficiency, she had a solid foundation that she was working from, and she had moved her entire business to the Cloud so she now had access to her business from ***anywhere, anytime and on any device.***

Working in the Cloud was incrementally giving Justine her time back and she was feeling good about things. Now some weekends at least were spent hanging out with her partner and little boy instead of catching up on the dreaded admin.

Then an opportunity arose to secure some contract work that was going to provide a steady revenue stream outside her coaching business. This meant having to work with a team, spend some time each week in an office, and it also involved travel.

It was a great opportunity, but it would mean juggling her time between her coaching business, the contract work and of course her family life.

It didn't take long for Justine to end up back on a seven-day workweek, and she called me to share her frustrations about it.

I asked her to send me a snapshot of her typical day so we could discuss it in our next one-on-one session.

This is what Justine came back with:

> "I've been arriving at the office nice and early to try and get a head

start before the team arrives. My first mistake is opening my email first. Somehow there are 50 new emails that have arrived overnight, unbelievable. These get added to the 150 still sitting in my inbox that I haven't dealt with yet.

"I work through, knocking over as many of these as I can so I can get to the work I had prioritised for the day.

"Time flies and, before I know it, the team starts turning up. The next hour or so are spent working through each team member's individual problem. Quick questions turn into long discussions and more items being added to my to-do list.

"I spend the rest of my morning fielding incoming client and supplier calls and adding even more items to my ever-growing list, and then lunchtime comes around and I have to cancel a lunch date with a friend. Instead I grab a takeaway from the café on the corner, eat at my desk and keep working.

"The afternoon is pretty much the same as the morning, I manage to tick two or three items off my list, but I mostly add more than I tick off.

"My plan to get away at 5pm fails.

"Today has been a good day for business though. The team signed up some new clients, which is fantastic, although I really don't know how we're going to manage the additional workload.

"I still have to get home, spend some time with Nash and Darren, organise dinner, and tonight I'm committed to a Chamber of Commerce meeting at 7:30pm.

"Andy, putting that down on paper really has me starting to question why I decided to go into business and then also take on contract work.

What was I thinking?"

I wasn't at all surprised by what Justine had shared. It's pretty similar to a day in the life of many a business owner.

I decided that maybe our next one-on-one session should be face-to-face rather than a Zoom.

> "So, Justine, you shared a typical day for you. I notice it was a day where you do your contract work in the office. What's happening with your coaching business though?"

> "Well, that's the problem. New business has dropped off and I'm struggling to manage my existing clients. The contract work is great as a regular means of revenue, but leadership coaching is where my passion is. There are not enough hours in the day to do everything and I feel like I'm in a rut. Income is coming in, but at the expense of my time and, in a way, my passion and purpose."

> "Okay, so you need both in your life from a financial point of view, but we should work out how you can manage them. Are the hours for the contract work locked in? How many days are you committed to?"

> "Yes, I'm locked in for three days a week."

> "Okay, so that leaves only two days for your coaching business."

> "In theory, but I'm spending the other four days of the week on it, and nights too. It's so tiring."

> "Well, let's work on what we can control — the coaching business. Do you have a set process for getting new clients, onboarding them and then working with them?"

> "You could say that. It follows a similar path, but with some variances for

each client. Sometimes it depends on how much time I have. The follow-up and support in-between sessions can be very time-consuming".

"Are there parts of the process that you enjoy and other parts not so much?"

"I love the face-to-face with the clients and the workshops that I sometimes get asked to present. These are the things I really love. The follow-up, writing reports and, as I've mentioned before, the admin — I don't really love."

"Is this process documented?"

"Gosh no, it's all in my head. I don't have time to document it, and besides I'm the only one that needs to know how to do it."

"Therein lies the problem. While you may be the only one that needs to know how to do it right now, that may not necessarily always be the case. What if you could set it up so someone else could take some of the workload off your shoulders?"

"That would be awesome. Not sure how that's going to work though."

"We just need to get those processes out of your head, and then we can make that happen."

"Okay, if you say so. I'll try anything to get out of this situation."

I now had Justine onboard. Justine had made the decision to start **getting the processes out of her head.**

One of the main barriers that prevents business owners from systemising their business is they think that their business has nothing that can be systemised.

But there are systems all around us. Every part of life is a system.

Our health and wellbeing are a system. What we eat, when we eat, when and if we exercise — if we follow a good system we end up with a good result, and our health and wellbeing benefit.

We follow documented and undocumented systems unconsciously every day, just by doing certain things the same way every time to make our life easier. Putting our car keys in the same place every time (or not, then not being able to find them. Sound familiar?), recipes we follow to make our favourite dishes, even our bathroom routine. Doing things the same way every time removes the need to make decisions.

The very same can be said for creating systems in your business. It's all about creating consistency and removing the need to spend time making decisions.

Your business is made up of tasks and processes that can be systemised much more than you may realise.

The other barrier to business owners documenting their processes is that documenting everything sounds like an enormous job, overwhelming.

You may very well, like most business owners, feel most of the things you do can't be systemised or you don't have time to document your processes. You're too busy, and it's easier, or you think it's much easier, to do it yourself.

Systemising a business doesn't sound like much of a fun thing to do, and, yes, life is busy, and, yes, it is easier to do some things yourself, but that's the very reason you are so busy.

Justine wasn't convinced yet.

> "Andy, I've had a bit of a think about this and I'm not sure there is much in my business that can be systemised. Most of the stuff I just do."
>
> "I can see you've been talking yourself out of this one."

"Ha, you're probably right there."

"I want you to do an exercise for me. Let's just focus on your client process. Create a project in Asana, name it Client Process Template, visualise everything you do as part of your client process, from client enquiry right through to working with the client over time. Add each part as a new task in the project. It doesn't need to be perfect, you can keep adding to it as you go, and you don't have to do it all in one session."

"Okay, I can do that. That's not too hard."

"Fantastic. Don't overthink it or get ahead of yourself. I'll send you the step-by-step tutorials on what to do next."

"It still sounds like a lot of work."

"It may seem like that now, but you only need to do it once, then you'll be set to have a process that you or someone else can follow and repeat with ease by simply duplicating the template."

"If it gets me away from this seven-day week and gives me my family time back, I'm up for it."

"Sounds like a plan then. Get to it, and I'll send you a link to the tutorials."

Concerned like Justine? Don't be. I made a promise of simple systems upfront in this book.

The process I'm about to share is a template for creating consistency in every system you build into your business. Once you have it mastered, you hit repeat.

A few tips before we start.

- Aim to build and refine. Initially your documentation may not be perfect. That's okay. Updating and improving is part of the process.

- You can and should involve your team.

- If you haven't done it already, now is the time to sign up for Asana. It's what we'll be using from this point forward right through to the Step 5 chapter. Asana will become the engine room for your operations, and it will help calm the chaos, save you time and become one of the main tools that enables you to operate your business from anywhere.

- You can access the detailed step-by-step tutorials on the **WFA Systems Build & Action Flow** at *https://wfa.life/resources*

Here is the overall workflow that we will be working through to get the processes out of your head:

The WFA System Build Flow

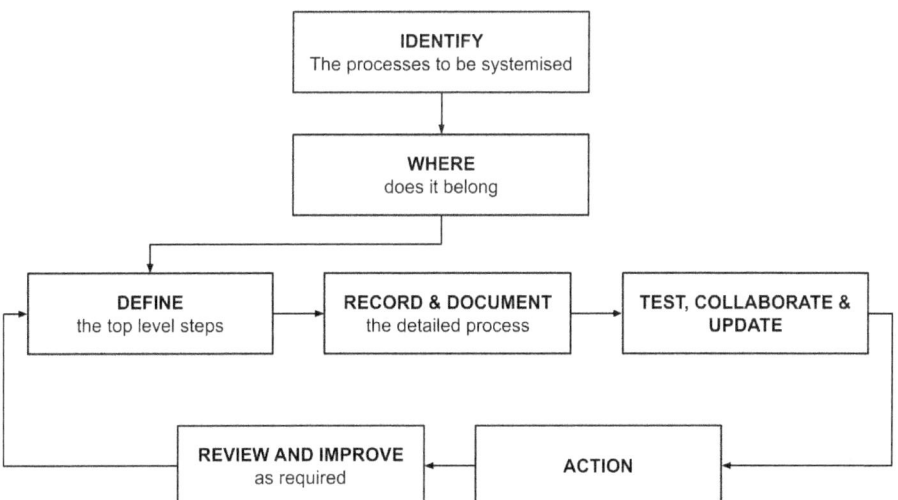

Systems Build Step 1 - Identify

You first need to identify the processes that can be systemised. Start with some of the most frequently used processes. Try and pick some that are easy wins.

Here are some examples:

- Sales process - the full process from sourcing clients/customers to product delivery
- New team member onboarding process
- How to create an invoice (very important)
- Social media marketing process
- Company communication policy
- Business opening procedure
- Business closing procedure.

Do it all as a brain dump. Start building a list that you can add to. It doesn't matter if you don't document or create a system for every process. This list will provide you with the opportunity to assess and prioritise what to systemise.

Continuing to add to this list as you think of things, or better still when you carry out a task or a process, gives you something to work with in the future.

Don't hold back. Just getting all the tasks and processes out of your head and into the one place will make you feel better.

Here's where using Asana comes in, this is the start of the **WFA Systems Build & Action Workflow.**

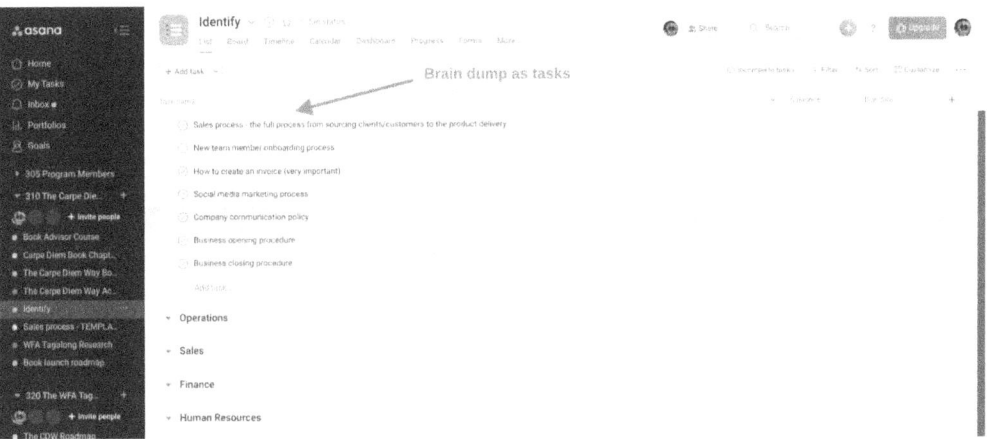

Create a project in Asana and name it, Identify, then start brain dumping your tasks and processes as tasks in the project.

Systems Build Step 2 - Where

Next you need to refer to the *accountability map*

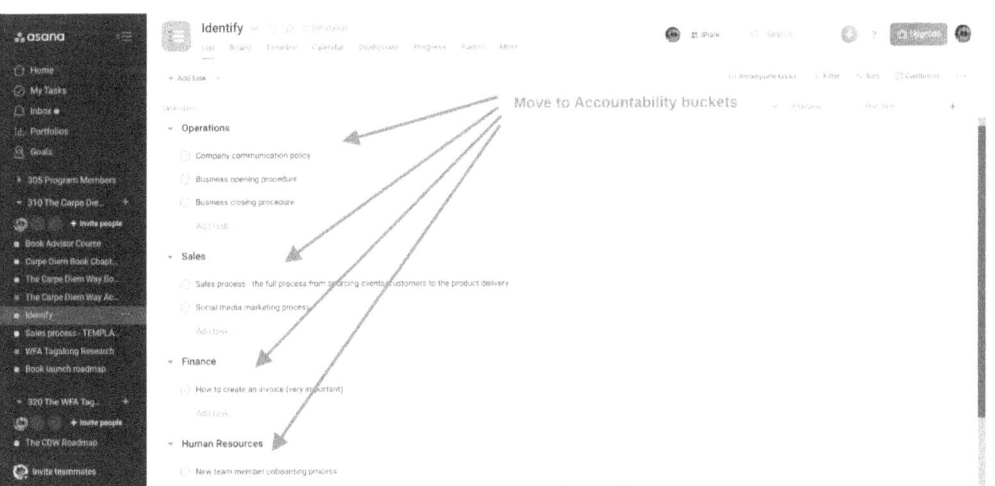

Create sections for each of the accountability buckets and move the items to the relative area/bucket of accountability.

Systems Build Step 3 - Define

The next step is to define the top-level steps of that task or process.

There will most likely be detailed steps within each top-level step. At this stage we are only looking at the very top level. Let's use the Sales Process as an example

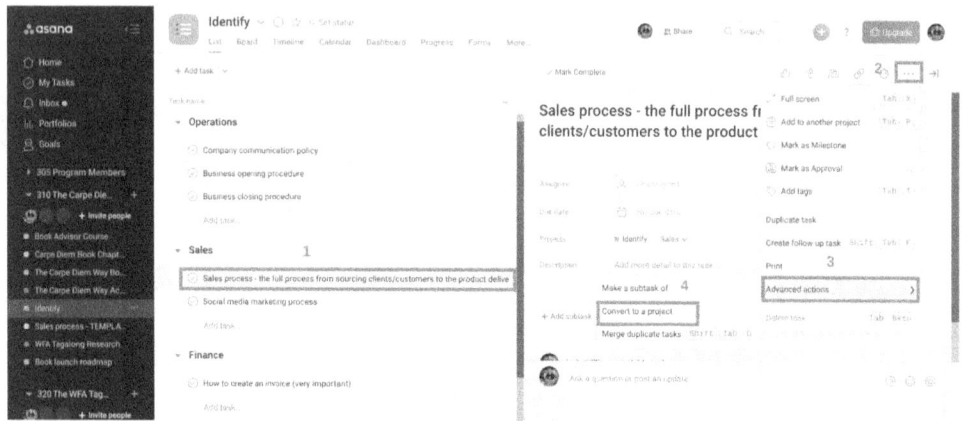

Select the Sales Process and change it from a task to a project.

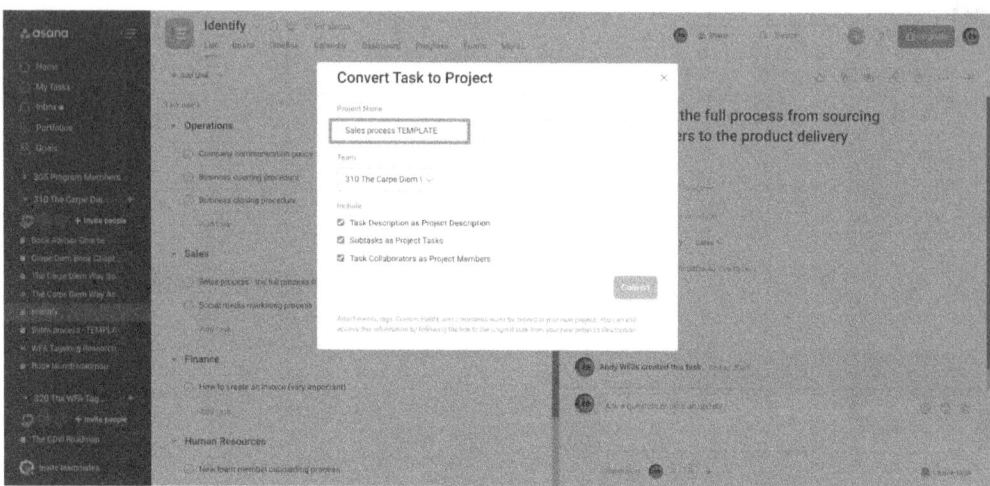

Rename it Sales Process TEMPLATE.

You are now ready to start populating it with the top-level steps of the sales process.

Let's use Justine's sales and client onboarding process for her leadership coaching business as an example. The top-level steps could be:

- Marketing and advertising channels
- Customer first contact methods
- Discovery call
- Create and send proposal
- Follow-up proposal
- Sign-up and payment
- Initial client session
- Create and send session report and program ongoing instructions.

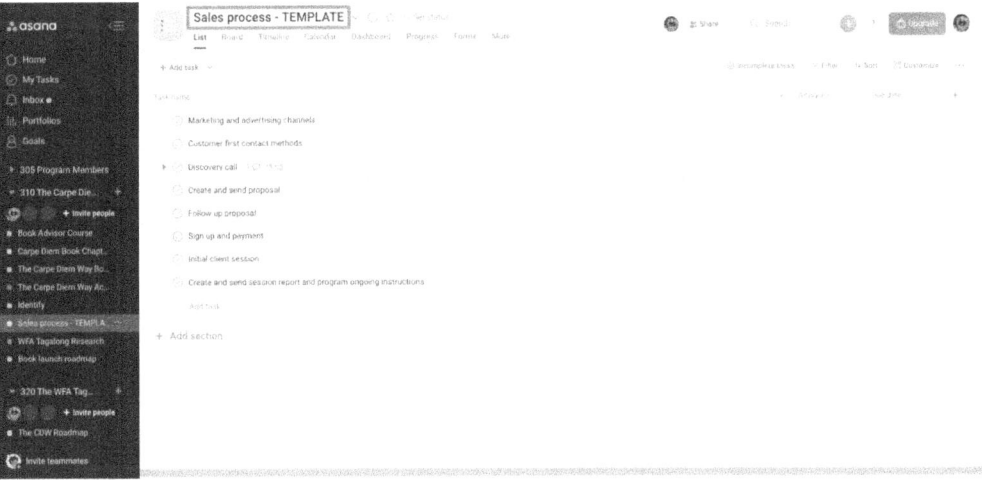

Add these as tasks in your Sales Process TEMPLATE.

Systems Build Step 4 - Record & Document

The next step is to record and document each of the processes in the top-level steps. How much detail you go into here is up to you. You may be happy with just having the top step for now. You can always expand on it at a later date.

Recording and documenting doesn't necessarily need to be done as text. Video is a great option.

Here are some examples of how to use video to record your processes:

- Demonstrate physical tasks in your business, such as walking through opening and locking up procedures using your mobile phone

- Create screen share recordings of how to do computer tasks and processes, such as processing an invoice in your accounting package - use Loom

- Client videos such as a coaching video that can be used for multiple clients - use Loom or your mobile phone.

I use a tool called Loom for demonstrating processes that are done on a computer. It's a great tool for recording screen share demonstration videos — easy to use and no editing needed. It's simply a matter of pressing record, and the video is saved and rendered in the Cloud. As soon as you hit the stop button you receive a link to paste into your process.

I use Loom to produce all my step-by-step tutorials in online programs, and couldn't live without it.

To document the processes, go to the Sales process - TEMPLATE.

STEP 3 - GETTING THE PROCESSES OUT OF YOUR HEAD | THE **CARPE DIEM** WAY

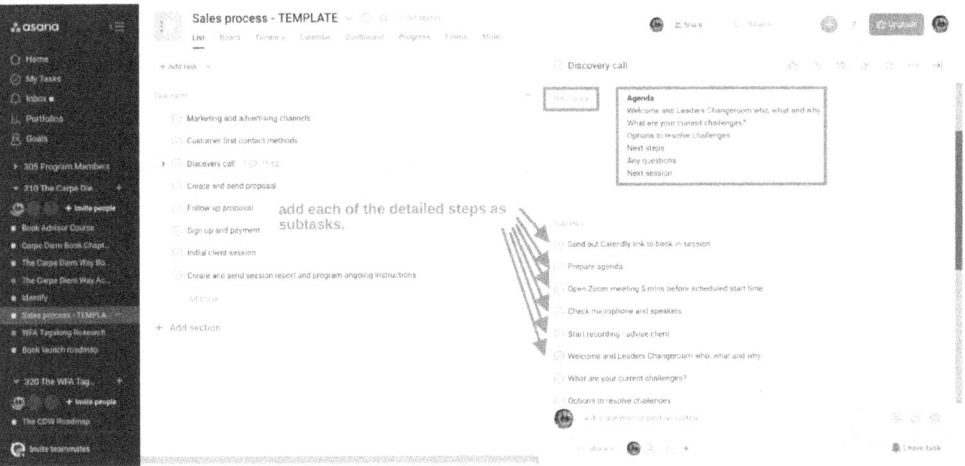

Using the discovery call as an example, click on the discovery call step and add each of the detailed steps as subtasks.

The main aim is to have everything related to the discovery call in one place.

You are not only *getting the processes out of your head,* you are building a template at the same time. These templates will flow through to be used in the *Step 4 Day-to-day operations from anywhere* chapter, where we move from how to do things to who does what and when.

Trust me, this will all make sense as you work through the **WFA Systems Build & Action Flow**. It really does flow.

Systems Build Step 5 - Test, Collaborate and Update

Now the task or process has been recorded and documented, the next step is to test the process. The best way to find gaps is to ask someone unfamiliar with it to work through it based on your documented system.

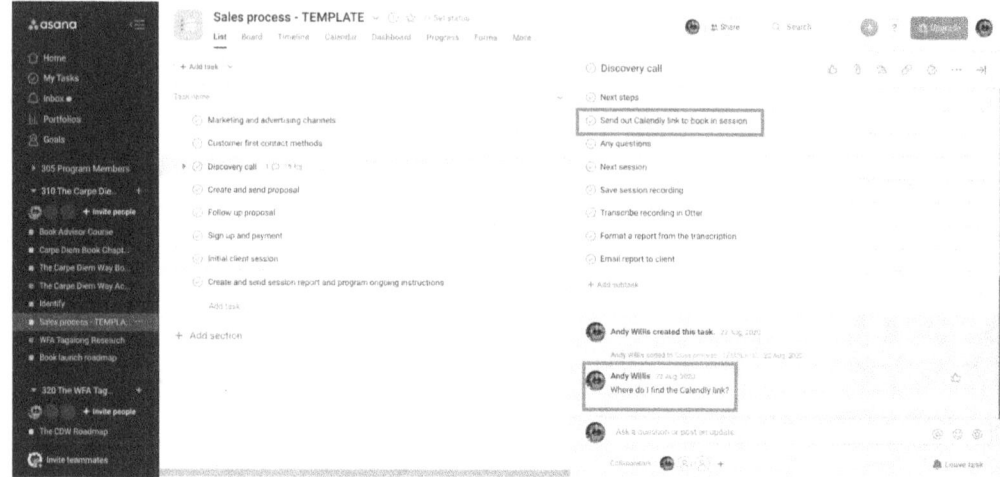

Ask them to add notes on the relevant step as they work through the process. This keeps everything related to each step in one place.

Continue collaborating on the process with the tester, updating based on feedback, until the process is completed by following the updated steps.

Systems Build Step 6 - Action

Your system is now ready. This is the action part of the flow, covered in more detail in the next chapter.

Systems Build Step 7 - Review and improve continuously

This step is as important as any of others. It is not a set and forget process. Your systems are only as useful as the information in them, so if the information is out of date, then it may as well not be there.

Assign the responsibility for reviewing to the individual team members who perform each of the tasks and processes. They are the people who are most aware of any changes.

Also include improvements as part of this responsibility. The same people can add more detail to each of the systems as they perform the tasks.

These systems will be the backbone of your business, and make it run effectively, saving time and money. Continual review and improvement are essential.

Justine turned up to our next one-on-one session with a big smile, looking very pleased with herself.

"Hey there, you're looking somewhat happier than when we last met. You left not feeling too sure about this whole systemisation thing. What changed?"

"Andy, the first thing you asked me to do was what made the difference for me. I wasn't convinced that there would be much that could be systemised in my business, and I couldn't see the point in spending the time documenting things that I just do without thinking.

"But you said to just brain dump everything I do into Asana as I either did it or thought about it, and then go over each item to see if it could be broken down into steps.

"So that's what I did. I did a brain dump and then kept adding to it as I went on. I then allocated some time one afternoon to go through the list and see if any of the items could be broken down into steps.

I was really surprised at how much of what I do could actually be broken down into steps."

"Okay, so did you move through to recording and documenting any of your processes as well?"

"Yes, I certainly did, and what happened was I discovered that I'm really inconsistent with some of my processes, in particular with my client workflow.

"Having to document the process forced me to think about each step and refine parts of the process. It was so helpful. I now have a clear set of steps I've tested, and I'm using the exact same process with every client.

"Wow, Andy, it's saved me so much time, and I'm getting great feedback from my clients. I've also picked up some great new clients because I've had more time to put into sales."

"That's awesome news, Justine. I'm so happy for you. You've now set up the platform that will take you to the next level."

"Oh really, there's a next level? I'm pretty happy with this one."

"You've done the hard work, so the next level is easy. It gives you back even more time."

"Wahoo! I'm not even going to question you anymore. I can't wait."

Justine had succeeded in **getting the processes out of her head,** and by now you too should be on the way.

It was onto the next step for Justine, and for you too now.

SUMMARY AND ACTIONS

The tools - Asana, Loom

The simple systems - The WFA Systems Build & Action Flow. Processes identified, recorded and documented. Use your Accountability Map

The mindset - Systemising areas of your business doesn't need to be complicated, and you don't have to do it all at once or do it all yourself. There are more tasks and processes in your business that are able to be documented than you realise.

Actions to get to Step 3 - Getting the processes out of your head

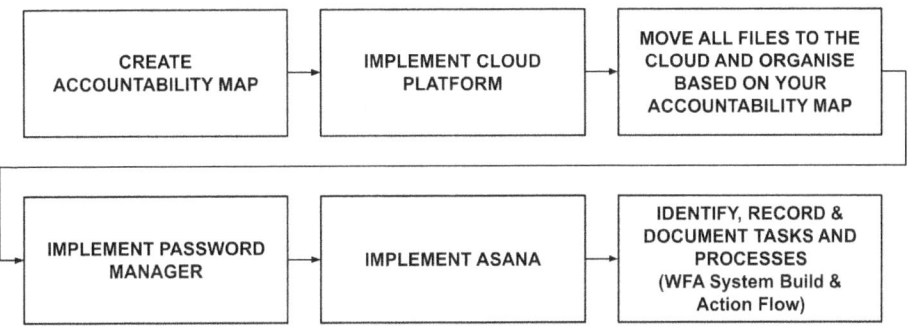

Check https://wfa.life/resources for more detailed information and access to step-by-step tutorials.

The Parable of the Mexican Fisherman

An American investment banker was taking a much-needed vacation in a small coastal Mexican village when a small boat with just one fisherman docked. The boat had several large, fresh fish in it.

The investment banker was impressed by the quality of the fish and asked the Mexican how long it took to catch them. The Mexican replied "Only a little while," and the banker asked why he didn't stay out longer and catch more.

The fisherman replied he had enough to support his family's immediate needs, and the American asked "But what do you do with the rest of your time?"

The Mexican replied "I sleep late, fish a little, play with my children, take a siesta with my wife, and stroll into the village each evening where I sip wine and play the guitar with my amigos: I have a full and busy life, señor."

The investment banker scoffed. "I am an Ivy League MBA, and I could help you. You could spend more time fishing and buy a bigger boat with the proceeds, and with the proceeds from the bigger boat you could buy several boats until eventually you would have a whole fleet of fishing boats. Instead of selling your catch to the middleman you could sell directly to the processor, eventually opening your own cannery. You could control the product, processing and distribution."

Then he added "Of course, you would need to leave this small coastal fishing village and move to Mexico City, where you would run your growing enterprise."

The fisherman asked "But, señor, how long will this all take?"

To which the American replied "15-20 years."

"But what then?" asked the Mexican.

The American laughed and said "That's the best part. When the time is right you would announce an IPO and sell your company stock to the public and become very rich. You could make millions."

"Millions, señor? Then what?"

And the investment banker said "Then you would retire. You could move to a small coastal fishing village where you would sleep late, fish a little, play with your kids, take a siesta with your wife, and stroll into the village in the evenings where you could sip wine and play your guitar with your amigos."

"But I'm already doing that," said the fisherman.

The now enlightened banker walked away pensively, with no trace of pity for the fisherman, only a little envy. The fisherman is living The Carpe Diem Way.

> "Happiness, not in another place but this place...not for another hour, but this hour."
>
> Walt Whitman

ANDY'S STORY

Saying yes to new adventures

What started with a one-month stint in the French Alps in 2013, became two months in 2014, followed by three months in 2015, and I've continued to spend up to three months there every year since then.

Every year I stay in the same village. I have no desire to travel. For me it's about immersing myself and becoming part of the local community, and that's exactly what happened and continues to happen except for 2020 and we all know why.

It's not a holiday, and it's not work. It's my life.

My friendship with Lionel continues, the French lessons no longer formal, more a part of the activities we share: hikes, cafés, local events and BBQs with friends.

My new French friends are patient and understanding about my less than understandable grasp of their beautiful language. Much of the time my attempts at conversing with them are a form of light entertainment.

Lionel kept suggesting that maybe I should join him on a little hike to discover something new.

My main activity had always been cycling — it was the passion that ticked off fitness, exploration and exhilaration. Hiking was not something I had done a lot of.

Eventually I agreed and swapped the bike shoes for runners and a backpack.

I well remember that first little hike with a pair of batons (walking poles similar to ski poles). Off we went to climb up to Les Sept Laux, a climb to some beautiful lakes I was led to believe.

It was absolutely breathtaking in so many ways — the scenery, the views, the animals, and then there was the climb — 1,000m up a rocky trail that took your breath away. I was very fit from hours of climbing on the bike, but this was something different, using different muscles and balance to hop from rock to rock up the steep inclines of this "little" hike.

It led to the discovery of a different beauty for me, another view and feel of the beautiful Alps, the quiet, looking down on the clouds, animals, flowers, wild berries and so, so many beautiful lakes.

I thought cycling in the Alps could not be beaten, and I'm not saying this was better, but it was different. It was yet another discovery.

And then this happened…

We were enjoying pizza and beers at the Café de Paris one evening after a hiking adventure, discussing what a fantastic day it had been, when Lionel said to me casually "I think you're ready to experience Via Ferrata."

"What is Via Ferrata?" I asked.

"We climb up a little mountain face attached to a cable. It's okay. It's safe."

Of course I said yes.

Kitted up with a harness and a helmet, I was all set to go. The first few metres were already scary. My heart was beating so fast, and I was no more than a metre or two up. I looked up at Lionel and asked "Are you sure I can do this?"

His answer was, as always, "Of course. It is safe. You are okay."

Onward and upward we went, my heart pumping overtime like never before. Then I looked down. Now that was a mistake. The river was at least 150 metres below, and my heart was telling me it was 10 times that.

No more looking down for me.

And then came the bridge. Not a bridge as we know it, not a solid structure to safely navigate to the other side of a gorge, no, this was a couple of long cables with random pieces of timber placed between them with big gaps in between, I mean big gaps of all sizes and two cables for handrails.

I looked at Lionel and I muttered something like "you've got to be kidding me?" maybe — probably — with an expletive or two.

Up goes the heart rate another notch. I step onto the first rung of the bridge, followed by another step and immediately the whole structure is swaying. What was I thinking?

I made it to the other side and took a few deep breaths to settle my heart rate. I actually felt quite proud of myself — chuffed and amazed I'd done something so out of my comfort zone.

Surely it can't get any scarier?

I could see the top. It was just there, but the rockface ahead was actually slanted backwards. How is this going to work, I wonder?

I suddenly became aware of the intense fatigue in my arms, supporting my whole body weight. The only thing that got me through was knowing I only had to hang on for another two metres. I could see the top… and I made it!

The feeling of exhilaration, triumph, excitement was like nothing I had ever experienced in my life. I jumped up and down and punched the air as though I'd conquered Mt Everest.

A few years ago if you'd asked me "Would you climb up a near vertical mountain face with a single cable the only thing between you and the ground hundreds of metres below?" I would have replied without hesitation "No way!"

I didn't have a bucket list of adventures. Life was simply offering up these amazing opportunities to really live. All I had to do was seize the day and say YES! to new adventures.

| Step 4
Day-to-day operations from anywhere

> "Doing less is not being lazy. Don't give in to a culture that values personal sacrifice over personal productivity."
>
> Timothy Ferriss, The 4-Hour Workweek

You've built a solid foundation for your business by creating an Accountability Map that is flowing through your operations, you've moved all your data to the Cloud and you're now using cloud-based software so you can access your business from **anywhere, at anytime, and on any device,** and in the previous step you started **getting the processes out of your head.**

The previous step was all about 'how to?' But in this step we move onto the 'who does what and when?' You may very well still be the who for many of the tasks, but now the processes are out of your head and into a system, you're in a great position to start delegating some of your workload.

If you need motivation to get you through some of these processes and new skills, check your notes again, where you listed the people and things that are important to you.

These strategies will improve your business for sure, but ultimately this

is about a better life and the strategies give you the opportunity to make time for life, to do what's important for you and for the people who are important to you.

Visualise what you want your ultimate day-to-day life to look like.

Believe me, things will happen that you never dreamt of. That's what happened to me, Justine and many others.

Okay, now you're motivated. Let's move on.

The WFA Systems Build & Action Flow (Action)

This step is the "Action" part of the **WFA Systems Build & Action Flow.**

We look at two strategies in this step:

1. Duplicating processes to streamline, create consistency and allow delegation
2. Managing your day-to-day to-do list and ad hoc tasks.

Duplicating processes to streamline, create consistency and allow delegation

This step will streamline the processes in your business, regardless of whether you delegate them or manage them yourself.

If you already delegate, this will make assigning tasks to your team easier and more effective. You will also be able to prioritise tasks and projects, monitor progress and provide support and feedback more easily from **anywhere, at anytime and on any device** with minimal interruption to your day.

Let's continue the flow of the Sales Process example we used in the previous chapter.

In the previous step we created a template for the full Sales Process. Let's put that template into action.

The scenario is a potential client who has booked in for a discovery call. We follow the sales process we created to give us the best chance of securing new business.

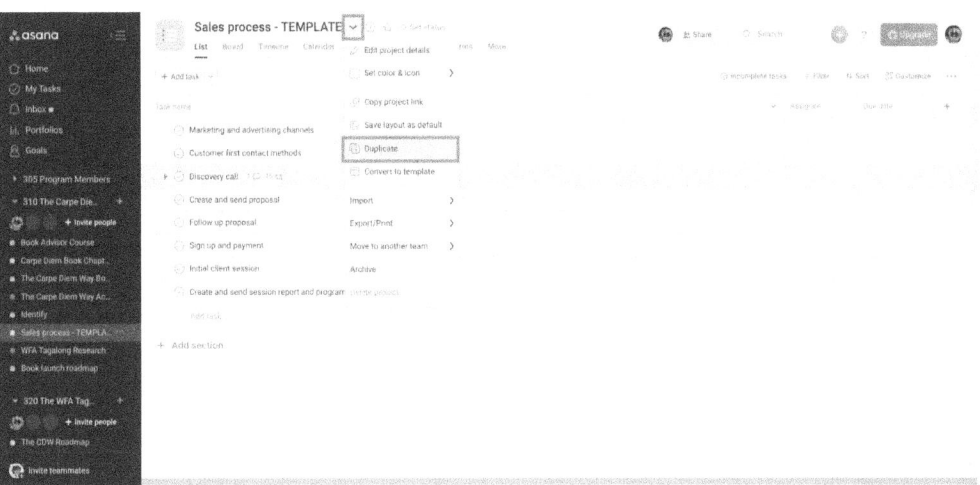

First go to the Sales Process TEMPLATE in Asana and duplicate the project.

(If you have created your own Sales Process in the previous step that is based on your actual process, even better, use that one)

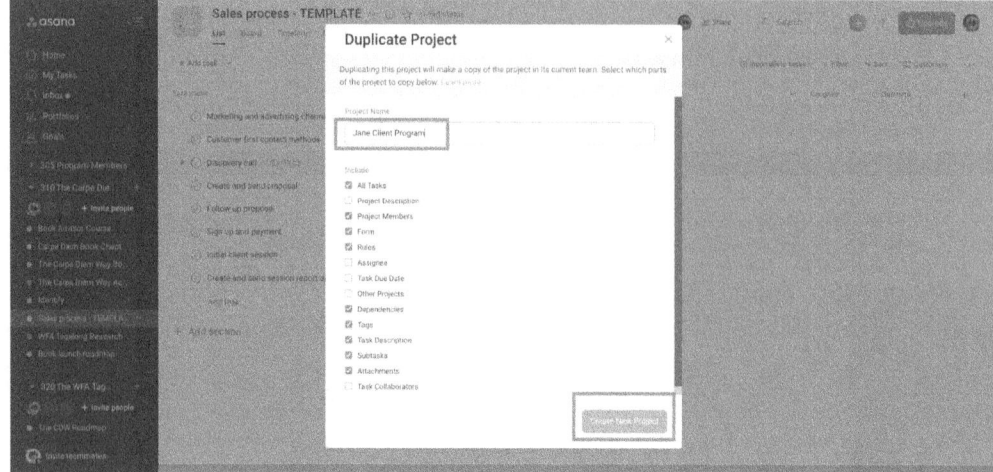

Rename the new project your client name.

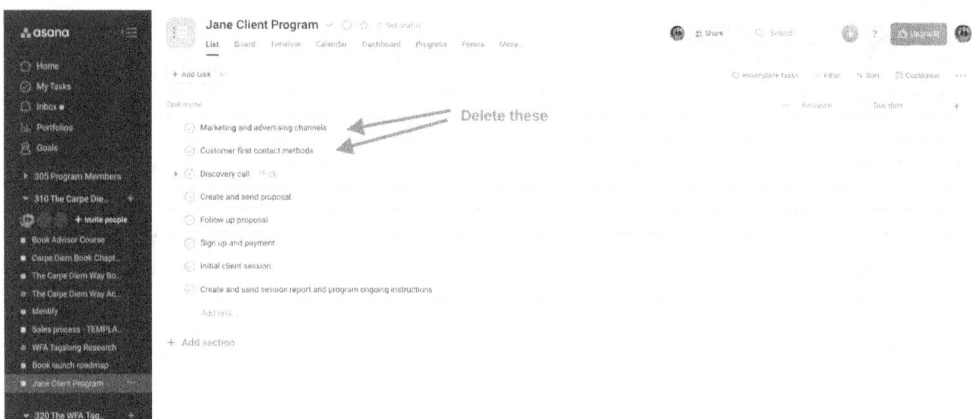

Delete the top two items as they have no relevance to the ongoing client process.

This leaves you with clear steps for working with your client, all achieved with minimal effort and without having to recreate the process from scratch every time.

Now you can assign and date each step.

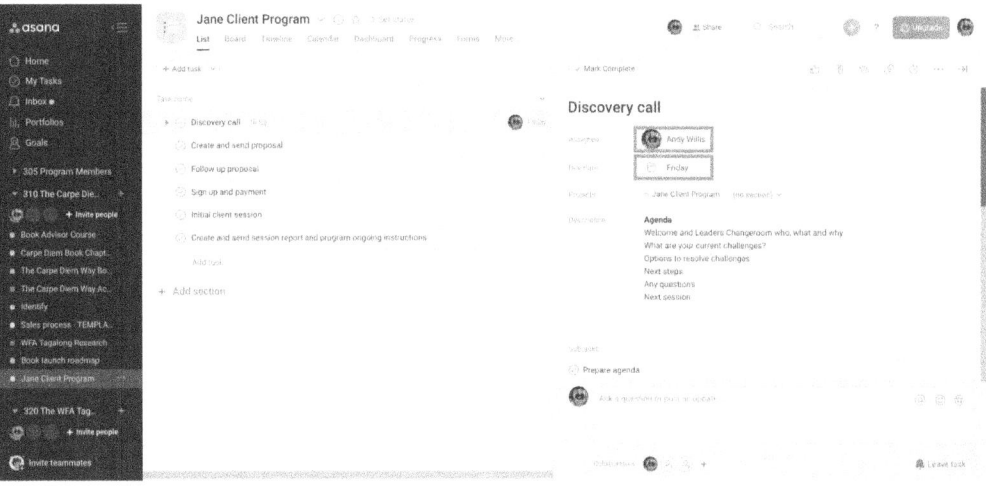

Assign and date the discovery call

You need to assign it to someone, even if that someone is you. Why? Assigning it to someone adds it to the assignees' "My Tasks" on the date you assign it, so nothing is missed.

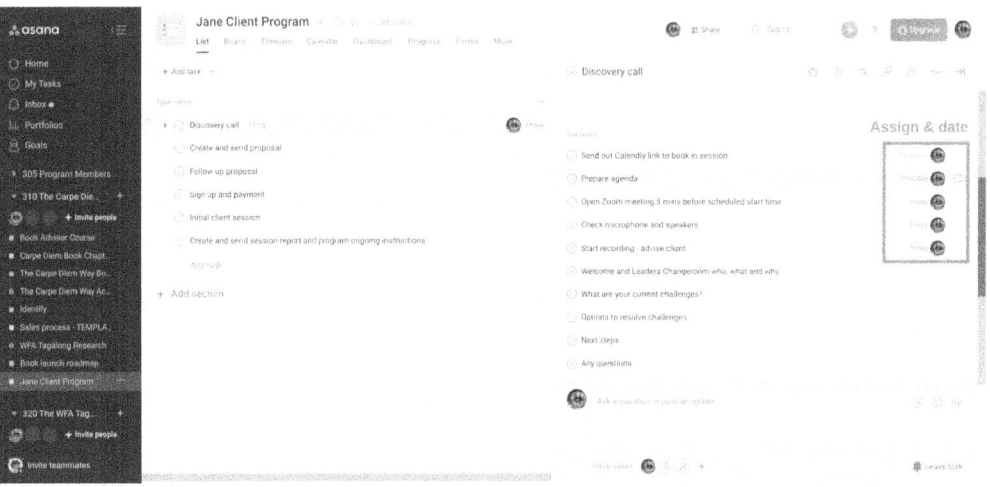

Now go into the individual subtasks which are your detailed steps, and assign and date where necessary.

That's it. The preparation items for the discovery call will now come up on the daily task list of the assignee on the due date, ensuring nothing gets missed. You can collaborate on each of the steps if necessary and monitor progress..

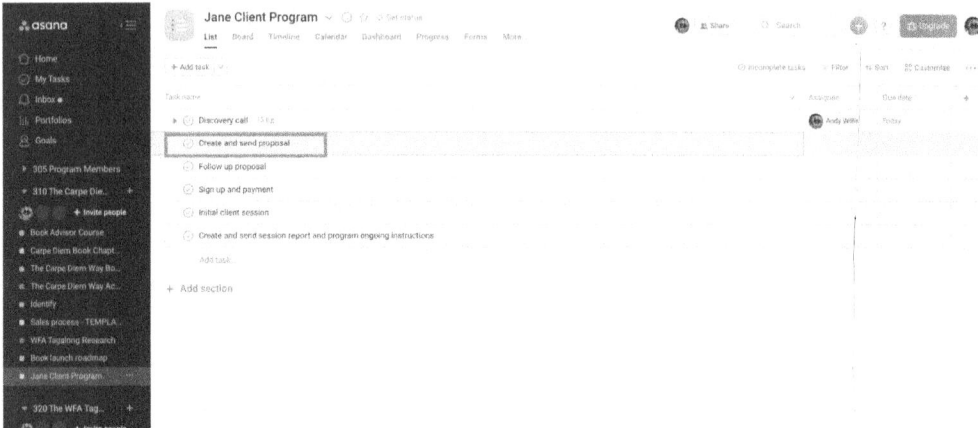

The discovery call happens, and you take notes during the meeting. Then you move to the next step of the client flow which, here, is creating and sending out a proposal.

That's it. Continue through the process, taking notes on the way. You can add documents, links, attach emails, reassign parts of the process or change dates if necessary. Everything to do with each part of the process can be found in the relevant place, so no searching for paper notes, text messages or in emails. Everything is in the one place, accessible from anywhere, at anytime on any device.

This same strategy can be used for every repeatable process in your business. No need to keep reinventing the wheel — simply duplicate, deliver and repeat.

You have now successfully put in place a procedure for *duplicating*

processes to streamline, create consistency and allow delegation that can be duplicated and repeated for every new client enquiry. You have created consistency, saved time and, hopefully, started delegating part of the process. You are using one core tool, Asana, and the **WFA System Build & Action Flow.**

Justine had fine-tuned her client process and started using templates to duplicate and repeat it effectively with each new client, but she was still struggling to claw back the extra hours and days that she needed to keep up with both the contract work and her coaching business.

> "Andy, I'm absolutely loving the client process. Being able to duplicate rather than create from scratch has saved me so much time. It's also making sure I follow the same process with consistency and don't miss anything. I'm still struggling to keep up with both the contract work and my business though. It gets really confusing trying to track and do tasks from both places. I have a massive to-do list for each."

"So you're not using Asana for your tasks?"

"I'm using Asana for my processes, and that's working really well, but I'm not using it for all the ad hoc tasks that pop up. I end up with all these things going around in my head — all the things I need to do for the two, actually three, parts of my life — the two businesses and my personal life. They keep me awake at night, and I wake up feeling more tired than when I went to bed."

"We need to change that. We've got your processes out of your head, and now we need to get the rest of the congestion out of there. The way to do that is by committing to using Asana 100% in your life. I know you're a list person, so we just need to give you a way to prioritise that list in a way that works."

"I've tried putting it all down on one list, but it's massive. It's overwhelming looking at the long list."

"That's a big part of the problem. We need to reduce the number of items you look at every day and to be realistic about how much you can achieve in one day, and only have that many items on the list."

"Sounds good, but what about everything else? How will I track the rest of the to-dos without missing anything?"

"I have a simple system for that, using Asana of course and a little discipline."

"Okay, lay it out and I'll give it a go."

I then walked Justine through my **managing your day-to-day to-do list and ad hoc tasks** process in Asana.

Just like Justine, every business owner has a to-do list, mostly a long, ever-growing one that, realistically, has no chance of ever being completed.

We set out with all good intentions by creating a to-do list, which could be a piece of paper, a whiteboard, a document or even a spreadsheet. To-do lists can work for you but, if you're not using them effectively, they may actually leave you feeling more disillusioned and stressed than you were before.

Most people find that general to-do lists don't work because:

- They get so overwhelmed just by looking at all the things they need to do

- They don't know how to prioritise the items on the list

- The easiest items on the list get tackled first and the hard ones either stay on the list, get moved to the next list or don't get done at all

- They feel that they are continually adding to their list but not reducing it
- There's a sense of confusion seeing home tasks mixed with work tasks.

Justine is not the only one with this problem. It's a challenge common to nearly every business owner I've worked with.

Gary and Jo have an award-winning oyster business. Their operation is spread over three physical locations: the oyster farm itself, a production shed and a shop front. These locations are far apart with different people working in different locations at different times.

Communicating and managing jobs between the locations was a real challenge: a mix of phone calls, text messages and separate whiteboards at each. It was clunky and far from productive.

Jo decided to participate in my Anywhere, Anytime, Any Device program, and was very enthusiastic.

The biggest breakthrough for her was using Asana to manage the day-to-day operations of their business over the three locations.

> "Amazing. I absolutely love Asana. It's completely changed the way we manage our operation. Everyone has embraced it, and it has made life so much easier.

> "We have some set processes in place that are working really well. What also works well is being able to create and assign tasks no matter where I am. I'm often out and about when I think of something that needs to be done, I just add it to Asana on my mobile and assign it to Gary or Sam. It's so easy — it's out of my mind and nothing gets missed anymore.

"I've also been using the voice to text option to add tasks all the time, which is so much easier than typing. Sometimes I just dump something I think of in Asana and then add detail and assign later.

"The strategy you shared on the program has been a game changer and I use it both in business and my personal life. I can't live without Asana now. Thank you so much, Andy."

Let's take a look at the strategy Jo implemented that was such a game changer. Justine implemented it too, with similar success.

It stops you from being overwhelmed, allows you to prioritise more effectively, reduces confusion and makes sure nothing is missed.

You've already implemented Asana by now, and I assume that you went through the Asana onboarding steps when you signed up, or worked out for yourself the basics of how the "Your Tasks" tab works.

Managing your day-to-day to-do list and ad hoc tasks.

It's a simple one-two strategy:

1. Add tasks from anywhere, at anytime and on any device
2. Prioritise your "My Tasks" twice a day.

1. Adding tasks from anywhere, at anytime and on any device.

You can add tasks into Asana from a browser or a mobile device, or even straight from your inbox. You can also use the voice to text option, just like Jo does. Very handy.

I encourage you to get into the habit of brain dumping into Asana whenever you think of something. Just create the task with minimal details, and then

you can add details, prioritise and assign later.

This will reduce some of your stress, and free your mind up to focus on the job at hand rather than being tempted to multitask. Switching from task to task achieves very little.

Getting these things out of your head, and knowing they won't be missed also helps you sleep at night.

2. Prioritise your "My Tasks" twice a day

The second part of this strategy takes some discipline: the prioritising of your "My Tasks" at the beginning and towards the end of your work day.

Here's an example of how we do this:

We're going to start at the top and work down.

All the new tasks you have added to Asana from your mobile or when someone assigns you a task get added to the "Recently Assigned" section of your "My Tasks" tab.

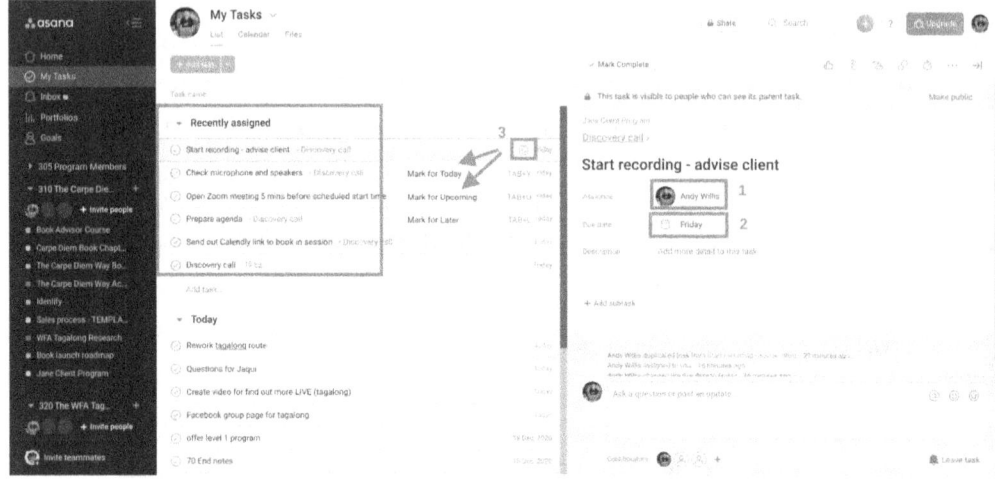

1. The first thing you need to do is reassign the task if necessary or leave it assigned to yourself

2. Then add a due date to the task. Most importantly, be realistic with the due date, otherwise you will be no better off. Also, add any additional details

3. Finally, move the task from recently assigned to "Mark for Today" or "Mark for upcoming". If you mark for today it will move down to your Today section, or if you mark it for upcoming it will move down to the Upcoming section and will automatically move up to your today section on the due date. Please note, even if you add a due date of today, you still need to mark it for Today.

Next move down to the Today section.

Here you will find any of the tasks you have just marked for Today and also any tasks that have moved up from the upcoming section because they have a due date of today.

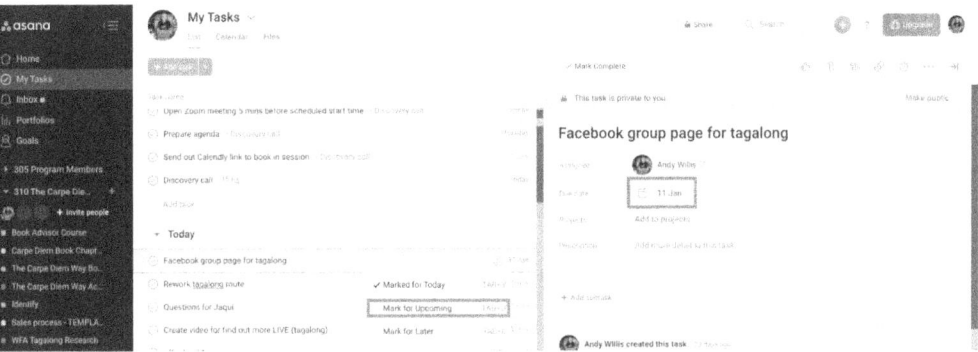

Now here is the most important part of this process: you assess and prioritise all of the items in this section so that there is a **MAXIMUM of six items.** You need to make the right decisions here: what are the most important six things that you can realistically achieve today?

> **"Things don't matter equally.**
>
> **Success is found in doing what matters most."**
>
> The ONE Thing by Gary Keller

Leaving only six items in this section removes the distraction and temptation to get side-tracked or start multitasking.

You also experience the joyful feeling that comes with ticking off that final item on your to-do list more often.

(Bonus - Asana has an animated unicorn that flies across the screen every time you tick off a number of tasks)

Think back to that list that had 50 items on it, and how overwhelming and stressful it was just to look at with no idea what to do next.

Leaving only six items on the list will give you focus. If you happen to

finish them all early, fine, add another or, preferably, reward yourself with a break

The process is the same as in the Recently Added section.

Assign, change date and Mark for Upcoming or leave in Today section.

Now start working on the highest priority task, ticking it off as you complete each one.

Repeat the same process towards the end of the day, by when you will probably have new items in the recently added section that need to be prioritised.

That's it. Repeat the same process twice daily.

It does take some time and discipline to make this a habit, but I assure you it's well worth it.

If you're at home but can't help thinking of things you need to do at work, you're going to miss out on being present with your partner, your kids or your friends. All those thoughts will keep you awake at night.

If you dump your thoughts into Asana, it frees your mind to be present and get some much needed sleep.

Your business foundation is now in place, and you've moved your entire business to the Cloud so you have access to everything from anywhere, anytime and on any device. You have got the processes out of your head and you've set up your business to manage your day-to-day operations more effectively. The next big step is physically stepping away from your business and letting go, one of the biggest challenges that many successful business owners face.

Letting go — truly delegating — is the next step in your transition to setting up your business to operate working from anywhere, the next step to living The Carpe Diem Way.

Hang in, we're just about there. Remind yourself again why you're doing this.

Onward to the next step in making **TIME** for **LIFE!**

SUMMARY AND ACTIONS

The tools - Asana.

The simple systems - The WFA Systems Build & Action Flow. Duplicate and repeat processes, managing your day-to-day to-do list.

The mindset - Multitasking is not productive, it's okay to have a short to-do list.

Actions To Get To Step 4 - Day to Day Operations From Anywhere

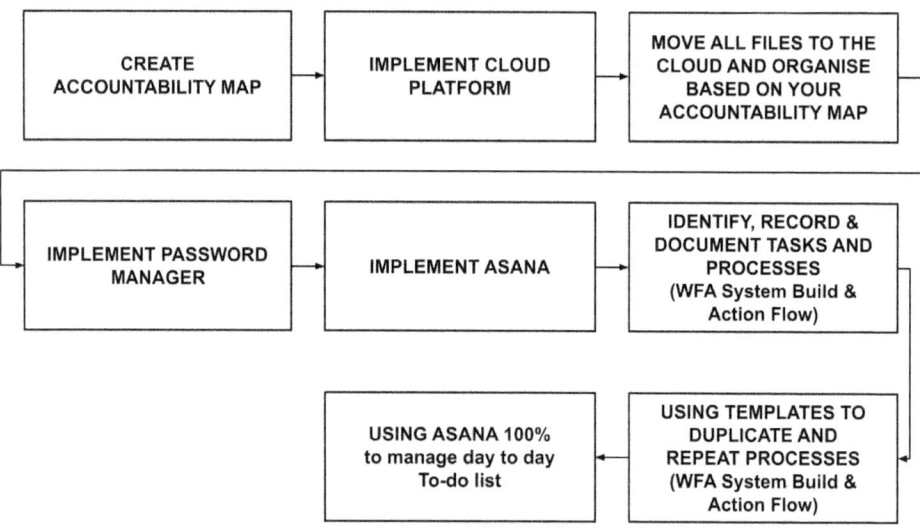

Check *https://wfa.life/resources* for more detailed information and access to step by step tutorials.

ANDY'S STORY

Sharing my French Alps life

The French Alps had created so much joy in my life that I started feeling a strong desire to share the experience with others so they too could discover joys of their own.

I had started a cycle tour business in 2012, Cyclerides Australia, a venture that combined my love of cycling with my experience as a travel and events professional.

So I put together The Taste of The Tour de France Tour cycling package that would run at the same time and in some of the same locations as the Tour de France, and engaged a cyclist friend of mine to lead the 2012 and 2013 tours as I had conference commitments.

Ten guys from Wagga Wagga, a city in the Riverina region of New South Wales, Australia, signed up for the 2014 tour, which fitted in perfectly with my two-month stint in the French Alps.

I've never seen 10 guys so excited, so enthusiastic for adventure and the local culture. They climbed every mountain I put in front of them, mixed with the locals, embraced French village ways and didn't mind finishing the day with a beer or two.

They were there to have fun!

It was more than a business venture for me — it was an opportunity to share the glorious French Alps and the beauty, joy and culture that had captured my heart.

From then on each year was a mix of leading a 14-day cycle tour and spending the rest of the time working on my conference business.

And, the cycling tours were funding my time in France!

Winning!

That same year someone new to my life, Jennie, joined for a while. Jennie wasn't a cyclist, but she could ride a bike, so we hired a bike, packed it in the van and drove up Alpe d'Huez so she could experience the exhilarating downhill.

That was enough to hook her on cycling and the French Alps at the same time, enough for her to take up cycling and want to return to the Alps several times in the years that followed.

2014 was just the start of sharing the beauty, joy, excitement and culture of French Alps with other people.

In the following years, Steve and Jemma, two cyclists who live close by, joined me for a private three-week guided cycling stay, Steve and Kathie, conference clients who had become good friends, stayed for some time in the village, my daughter Aleisha and her boyfriend Josh visited for five days as part of their big European adventure, Gary and Jo from Tathra joined us at the same time, and more cycling groups followed. My sister Karen came over from Bali and helped with the cycling groups, and Kathie and Steve even decided to stay on as support crew for the cycle tour.

Everyone went home with a little bit of the French Alps in their hearts and memories.

The mountains and culture drew Karen in so much that she returned and held her own retreat groups in the French Alps there as part of her active lifestyle business.

I've experienced the joy of sharing my French Alps' home, community and the climb up Alpe d'Huez with upwards of 80 family, friends and

customers over the years. The flexibility of the WFA strategies and mindset shift allowed me to be there and spend quality time with my visitors and customers throughout their stay.

The opportunity to share the French Alps with so many people was not planned, it was a bonus that I had never really considered when I started my WFA life.

It showed me that a joy that is shared is a joy that is much more than doubled.

| Step 5
Make TIME for LIFE

"There is no such thing as work-life balance. There is only life."

Andy Willis, WFA.life

It's time for the final step, the step where you will make TIME for LIFE.

This step is the final step to living The Carpe Diem Way.

In this chapter I share a simple strategy that takes delegation to the next level, and share options to effectively outsource to freelancers and external contractors.

Let's check in on your journey and what you have accomplished so far.

1. You have built a solid foundation and have an Accountability Map flowing through your operations

2. Your entire business is now secure in the Cloud and using cloud-based software

3. The processes are out of your head and you've built the systems and processes that allow other people to manage most tasks in your business

4. You're managing day-to-day operations effectively and your daily to-do list is no longer overwhelming

5. You and your team are able to monitor and collaborate on tasks and projects from anywhere

6. Hopefully you're already spending some time away from your place of business and making **TIME** for **LIFE.**

This step will allow you to free up even more of your time:

You now have the tools and simple systems in place, you're able to delegate tasks in Asana with ease, and you can collaborate on the same tasks in Asana.

You may still be struggling as we all tend to do with the burden of what we've been conditioned to accept as normal over many years of working life – the need to be there to deliver and delegate responsibilities and tasks to the team in person, the need to make sure they understand the importance of prioritising. Deadlines must be met, and some tasks are more time critical than others. What if they do the easy stuff first and leave the harder but higher priority tasks?

Physically stepping away from your business is one of the biggest challenges that successful business owners face.

But we're going to add the final touches that will set you up to push through this challenge.

In this chapter I share a simple strategy that will make delegation easier, more effective and able to be done from anywhere, at anytime, on any device.

The *anytime* part of this statement is of particular relevance, and you'll find out why as you work through the chapter.

This strategy is the same for working with your onsite team as for working external contractors and freelancers.

That's the whole point. We need to simplify life, and having fewer processes will achieve this.

Let's first take in some different scenarios:

- Your son has a sports carnival today and you've promised to watch him compete. He's really excited that you'll be there (this is pre-teenage so he's still happy for you to be around).
- You've booked an overseas holiday, but you have a project that needs your input and you'll be in a different time zone to your team.
- You've engaged a freelancer to do a website build, and they work to their own time schedule.

All of these scenarios involve you having to set up delegation and communication of tasks ahead of time.

The communication side of this is as important and sometimes more important than the delegation.

The simple strategy I'm about to share works for all of these scenarios, and the good news is that you already have everything in place.

Yes, that's right, no additional technical skills necessary for this one. You can use your newly acquired understanding from the previous chapters.

It's really is as easy as *1, 2, 3, rinse and repeat.*

Here is the simple three-step delegate framework:

Step 1

Set up tasks in Asana or use existing items, prioritise and assign the tasks to the relevant team member. Make sure the due dates are achievable.

Step 2

Next, film a short video for your team member or freelancer using Loom. Say good morning, just like you would if you were greeting them IRL, and share any additional details of the tasks you have set. You can demonstrate or explain using screen share if that helps add a little more clarity.

This is an important part of the process as it not only gives you an opportunity to clarify any details, but also adds the human element, keeping personal relationships alive and building up rapport with your team.

Not comfortable in front of the camera? No need to stress, you don't need a recording studio or fancy equipment and you don't need to be a movie star, many of the videos you create will not be for public viewing, others will be screen share only.

These videos should literally only take you a few minutes a day. You can share them as a link in an email or set up a Google Chat room specifically for this purpose.

Step 3

The team member or freelancer then works through the tasks, ticking them off and/or adding comments. They then record an end-of-day report with a quick Loom video. There is no need for these report videos to be long and detailed. It's all about keeping communication going from ***anywhere, at anytime and on any device.***

That's it, ***1, 2, 3 rinse and repeat*** daily or as needed.

So that's the simple strategy for working with your internal or external team.

Next let's talk about why and how to engage an external team member, something that, if done well, will give you another 20 hours a week or more — 20 hours a week that will allow you to make **TIME** for **LIFE.**

First up I really need to address one particular piece of terminology that makes me cringe every time I hear it: Virtual Assistant.

The outsourcing industry gave them the name Virtual Assistant or VA for short long ago, but what a dreadful term. These people are not virtual, they are real people with real skills that can add enormous value to your business.

They are valuable members of your team, no matter where they work from or who else they work with.

So, from this point forward I will refer to these skilful individuals as your global team members. Congratulations, you now have a global business. That's pretty cool, don't you think?

I'll let Justine share some very good reasons why you should consider engaging one of these good people.

Here is the actual transcript of a conversation I had with her on The Carpe Diem Conversation Show.

> "When you first started talking about a global team member, I dismissed it straight away. It's just me, and I'm not big enough. What would she do? She can't do what I do.
>
> "And then we had another couple of conversations, and I kind of reflected on that a little bit. And I thought, no, actually, I think I can

make this work. I'm good at delegating, because I've done that my whole life.

"Then I found out that I had to have her for a minimum of 20 hours a week. I was thinking five hours, you know, but that's not how it works. Twenty hours was the minimum. At the beginning I did struggle a little bit, because I didn't go in with enough ideas of what I could give her.

"But as it turns out the wonderful Mena is highly capable.

"Some of what I do is business planning, which requires researching the sector or the external market, Mena does a great job of this and it frees me up to do other stuff.

"I've got her to do PESTLE analysis and SWAT's. She does the groundwork and then I come in and refine it over the top and it's been amazing.

"And one of the biggest benefits of having her is the client experience: actually mapping out what support I can give to the client. What parts absolutely need me and what is just a follow-up or approach. So mapping that process out: will we contact them every week? What will we talk about? How we plan the next session. How do I give them feedback easily? How do we help them to be accountable and follow through on things, their commitments? Mena has been key to that because, as I said, she holds me accountable and she holds the process for me.

"So the clients are definitely getting a better experience.

"I engage her for 20 hours a week, but she probably gives me 30 hours a week to be honest.

"She does the administrative tasks much quicker than I would, and she's

doing them over and over again while I was doing them in-between things, so having to multitask and switch was difficult.

"And that's been a huge shift. Huge."

It was an amazing conversation with Justine, and you will find a link to the full recording on *htttps://wfa.life/resources*

It can be difficult to manage the change of mindset that is needed to let someone else take on some of your workload, breaking the conditioning of the past and managing trust and even guilt.

Now, you may have tried to engage a global team member before (btw global doesn't necessarily mean outside your country). Many business owners have, but most don't do it right.

The most common complaint from business owners is they end up not saving any time or it actually takes up more of their time.

Why? Because, unlike you, they don't have the systems and processes in place and they expect the global team member to know everything. They expect their new team member with zero experience in the business to know how everything works, and basically they expect them to be a mind reader.

So what happens?

This results in very poor outcomes for all concerned. The delegated tasks are not completed to expectations and have to be reworked time and again, and everyone is frustrated and unhappy.

It all gets too hard so the global team member is sacked because he or she doesn't know what they're doing, and the business owner reverts back to the old way of doing things because it's easier.

They really needed to read this book first.

This will not happen to you though, because you have the systems and processes in place and are already delegating tasks effectively. Delegating to your global team is no different to delegating to your local team.

Sourcing your first global team member

There are two main options, and picking the right one for your situation is important. The choices you have are :

- Go to one of the outsourcing platforms and look for a freelancer
- Engage the services of an outsourcing company.

What are the main differences between these options?

Outsourcing platforms such as Upwork, Fiverr and Freelancer, the main players, offer the opportunity to communicate directly with freelancers and organisations that have a team of freelancers. It's more or less the same as advertising an onsite position. You put out a brief and job description, and freelancers apply for your position and provide résumés, etc. You then communicate directly with the applicants to fill the position.

You sign off once you have agreed on terms, the number of hours, hourly rate, etc.

These platforms have systems in place to monitor when your team is working, and all payments to the freelancer go through the platform. It is against the contract to pay the freelancers directly or engage them outside the platform.

You are able to hire for a particular project based on an hourly rate or a fixed price quotation.

Using an outsourcing platform is a great option for one-off projects that

require a specific set of skills, and for getting assistance on an ad hoc or minimal hours' basis.

The other option is engaging the services of an **outsourcing company** with a pool of team members whom they hire, train and manage. Many of these organisations are structured for the sole purpose of providing fully trained general administration assistants to businesses and other organisations.

They also assist with the selection process, shortlisting based on the criteria you have provided. They then provide candidate résumés, skills, strengths, previous work experience and references for you to further narrow down the list for interviews.

The **outsourcing company** receives a monthly payment and they pay your team member, who may also be entitled to paid holidays and sick leave, both of which are part of your contract with the outsourcing company.

This option is ideal for engaging a permanent full- or part-time team member.

The major benefit of using an outsourcing company is that your global team member comes trained, and is supervised and supported and provided with the necessary equipment and software. These companies also provide tips and resources to assist you in working with your global team members.

The best of these companies also give their team members health care benefits.

One such organisation that I have used over the years is *The Virtual Hub,* a well-established outsourcing company with a pool of variously skilled team members.

Barbara Turley, founder & CEO of The Virtual Hub, is "an investor and

entrepreneur with a keen interest in scalable business models, systems, processes and automation, content marketing and the power of inspired and empowered teams".

Barbara said The Virtual Hub is "a business I started by accident that exploded in the space of 12 months to become one of the leading companies to recruit, train and manage virtual assistants for businesses which need to free up time and energy so they can go to the next level."

The Virtual Hub claim to, and I can attest that they do, provide the benefit of partnering with their clients to help them to prepare properly.

They recruit, hire, train, and mentor their own people and then pre-select 2-3 of their VAs to meet the client. Once the client chooses which one of the VAs they would like to work with they assign a Results Coach plus a Client Success Manager to the account. This 'pod' then services the account as a team to ensure ROI, growth & success for all.

A link to The Virtual Hub's full process can be found on the *https://wfa.life/resources*

The first thing to do once you've engaged someone is onboard them effectively, a very important and necessary step.

Onboarding and training your new team member

Onboarding a new global team member is virtually the same as onboarding a new onsite team member. That of course is if you already have your onboarding process in place, documented and available from anywhere, at anytime and on any device.

The only difference is that face-to-face discussions take place as video calls.

Working with your global team members

Once onboarded, use the process described earlier in this chapter to work with your global team member: *1, 2, 3, rinse and repeat.*

Keep in mind that communication is the key to success here, and each pre-recorded update and real time conversation is as important as the next.

They are part of your team, so make them feel that way.

Time to make TIME for LIFE

Engaging and delegating some of your workload either internally or externally are what will give you back your time to make time for life.

You will find the more you delegate, the more tasks you will feel comfortable with handing over until you hand over tasks that you thought no one but you could ever do.

One day you will be working away and suddenly realise that you have time — you have time and it's up to you what you do with this time.

This is your opportunity to take control and choose what you do with your time. Just like Justine, this is your opportunity to make TIME for LIFE by doing what's important to you, to the people in your life and to your business, preferably in that order.

This is living life *The Carpe Diem Way.*

SUMMARY AND ACTIONS

The tools - Asana, Loom, Google Meet or Zoom for video meetings

The simple systems - The three-step delegation process

The mindset - It's okay to delegate, and the more tasks you delegate the more you will find can be delegated.

Actions To Get To Step 5 - Making Time For Life

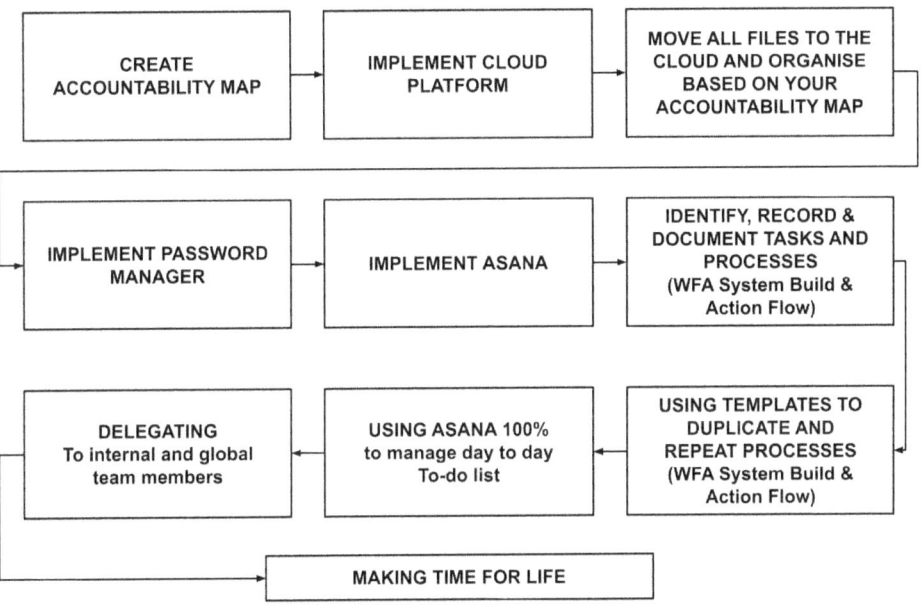

STOP!

Make TIME for LIFE.

As you know, I'm not a fan of bucket lists.

Too often they become the 'later' list, and sometimes later never comes.

You now have a list of the people and the things that are important to you and an idea of what an ideal day should look like.

By putting the Five Steps into place you have the tools, systems and mindset to make Time for Life.

It's time to prioritise and take action on your list.

It's your life. Your notes. Your ACTION PLAN.

Your chance to start living the Carpe Diem Way.

| My Carpe Diem Way

List the actions you will take so you can spend time with the people who count in your life and do the things that are important to you.

Be specific. Add dates, times, frequency and a budget if needed.

For example, if you aim to spend more time in the garden, say you will spend every XX day in the garden. If you intend to travel, add a date, destination and when you will book. Have an audacious goal that needs you to be in good shape healthwise? Maybe hiking Machu Picchu? Set a date for a training plan to get you there ready to hike.

_____

_____

_____

_____

_____

_____

_____

_____

"In playing ball, and in life, a person occasionally gets the opportunity to do something great. When that time comes, only two things matter: being prepared to seize the moment and having the courage to take your best swing."

Hank Aaron

ANDY'S STORY

WFA.Life was born

My time in the French Alps had become part of my life, part of who I am.

Every year, on my return home to Tathra I would be greeted by friends and colleagues with the question "How was your holiday?" and comments like "What a great life you have. You are so lucky."

People really struggled with the concept that it's not actually a holiday for me; it's my life.

We are so conditioned to believe that any time spent away from our place of work at a destination away from where we live, especially one as stunning as the French Alps, must be a holiday.

Many of these people are in exactly the same place I was back in 2012, running successful businesses and deferring living life until later. Their business is their life.

Seeing my friends and other business owners in this situation started to really bother me, and I wanted to help. I decided to make it my life purpose to help other business owners discover there is another way to live.

I had no idea how to do it, and definitely no idea how to make it pay. All I knew was that I wanted to do it. The message and inspiration were the important part, so surely if I got those right I could make a living out of it?

I was now in my mid-fifties, and this was my opportunity to give back in a thoughtful way, my opportunity to live a life with purpose.

Truthfully, I had never given any thought to having a purpose. I'd stumbled through life, giving little thought to why I was doing whatever it was. I just did it.

I decided I'd call this mission Working From Anywhere. WFA.Life was born.

WFA.Life has had many, many iterations over the years. It has been a long journey and a continual build of research, knowledge, resources and methods of delivery.

I've been very fortunate to work with many business owners over the years and witness the difference transitioning their businesses has made to their lives.

2019 was a special year, a year that I was able to bring together the best of what I do and what I love.

I invited program members to join me for a Carpe Diem Retreat in The French Alps. This was my chance to give people the opportunity to live what they had learned, and also share the place where WFA life started for me.

By early June I was back in my second home doing what I do: cycling, hiking, hanging out with my friends, enjoying village culture, and of course working from anywhere. My sister Karen, who has supported me through my entire WFA journey, joined me the week before the retreat.

The group arrived from various directions, at various pick-up points. The excitement and non-stop conversation on the drive to the village was like old friends seeing each other after a long time apart rather than people meeting for the first time.

Our 'gîte' (the French term for a vacation house typically found in a rural district) was just around the corner from my apartment in Le Vert. Les Petites Sources is a magnificent old house originally built in 1750 and restored in 1992 by owners and hosts Pauline and Éric. With mountain

views from the chalet-style bedrooms, a dining and living room in typical mountain style and lovely gardens, it was the perfect home base.

Each day started at the breakfast table laden with fresh local produce, the bread straight out of the local boulangerie oven. I'd planned morning workshop sessions, but soon found they turned into conversations on the mindset and life challenges that everyone had experienced working through the program, and the changes they had made to the way they worked and lived to get to this point.

A common factor for everyone turned out to be guilt.

The guilt of not being at their place of business for their staff to see, the guilt of spending too much time working and not enough time with family, the guilt of working irregular hours, the guilt of going to the gym or catching up for coffee during work hours, and even the guilt of being here in the French Alps while the team back home was running the business. This issue turned into heartfelt discussions throughout the week, with everyone vowing to work on letting it go.

On day 3 Lionel arrived at the hotel with several sets of walking batons, ready to lead the group on their first hike. I was confident the experience would blow their minds.

There were excitement and wows as we wound our way up the 21 hairpin bends of the famous Alpe d'Huez in the van. It was fantastic, and then they got to experience the thrill of being high in the Alps above the clouds as they hiked around Lac Besson and the adjoining beautiful lakes, and I could see the smiles on their faces, the exhilaration, freedom and peace that come with being in the rugged but glorious Alps.

Evenings became a regular pre-dinner drinks session at the local Café de Paris, followed by home-brewed aperitifs and an amazing five-course

dinner in the garden at Les Petites Sources. We enjoyed the very best provincial food and wine every day.

Everyone still got their work done, and ran their businesses while learning and living in another part of the world.

The week finished with an afternoon of champagne and reflection in the garden. It was hard to hold back my emotions as I recapped the retreat and farewelled a group of people who had created a lifelong bond over a very short period of time.

I'll never forget these words of gratitude from Justine:

"I had absolutely no idea that the retreat would have the magnitude of the impact it's had on me personally. I will be eternally grateful. You've basically shared your life with us. Not many people would do that for other people and you did."

I was always confident that the retreat would be a success, but I underestimated the level of emotion and the openness of the conversations.

So much came out of the retreat: collaboration, friendship, business clarity, reflections, goals, thrilling adventures, and so many good spirited laughs. I could write a whole book on the seven days — maybe next time.

I have never ever felt better in my life. This was a major milestone in delivering on my life purpose to help others discover **The Carpe Diem Way.**

Section 3

| The Time is Now:
Start living life The Carpe Diem Way!

> "In the end, it's not the years in your life that count. It's the life in your years."
>
> Abraham Lincoln

You have completed the five powerful steps to working from anywhere, so all that's left now is for you to start living The Carpe Diem Way, just like Justine did.

Justine transitioned from a seven-day workweek struggling to spend quality time with her partner and little boy, to setting off on a seven-week WFA caravan adventure around Tasmania. Equipped with tools, strategies and most of all mindset, Justine managed her growing business and explored Tasmania with her partner and little boy, discovering new places and meeting new friends along the way.

Her business continues to grow, but not at the expense of her family life, and as I write this chapter she is heading off on another four-week WFA caravan adventure, which will make 11 weeks so far this year. Justine has made a conscious decision to make this one two weeks' holiday and two weeks' WFA.

That is an important point right there: just because you can operate your

business from anywhere, at anytime and on any device it doesn't mean you're available 24/7. It's as important to still take holidays, completely switch off at times, and take a break and relax.

The Carpe Diem Way is all about choices and prioritising what's important to you every day.

So now it's your turn. Look back at your notes, your list of what and who are important to you, and how much time you would like to spend doing those things and being with those people. Now is the time to put everything into real-life practice. Now is the time to seize the day and make **TIME** for **LIFE**.

Take inspiration from the fact that Justine has moved from working a seven-day a week to a four-day week, a café and local produce store can be set up so the owner can visit overseas relatives every year, a timber industry business owner can spend up to two months at a time travelling every year, an organic skincare business can take regular caravan trips away to sell their products and an oyster farming family can spend winters up north.

These successful business owners are operating their businesses and earning a living as they experience life now. This is not work-life balance, this is life.

You're not trying to build a fast-paced start up. You have already built a successful business. This is about building a successful life. This is a long-term project, very long – the rest of your life.

There is no perfect starting point in your life.

Don't put it off, seize the day. ***Carpe Diem.***

| The Next Chapter

Then along came 2020 and a world event like none other, the COVID-19 global pandemic with its economic fallout, crisis at a scale not seen since the Second World War. It's been a year that gave every one of us pause to reflect on what is important in our lives.

Shops and businesses were forced to close, many millions were, and still are locked-down in their homes. Working from home became mandatory for all businesses rather than an option for the more progressive. The family home turned into the office and classroom while parents gained a new role, that of teacher support staff. Zoom becomes a way of life.

> **"Zoom has now revealed that it has surpassed 300 million daily Zoom meeting participants. That's up 50 per cent from the 200 million the company reported earlier this month, and a huge jump from the 10 million back in December."**

In the blink of an eye businesses and organisations that had resisted allowing their team to work remotely were forced to do so. Some managed the change much more effectively and with less pain than others.

Demand for the **Anywhere, Anytime, Any Device Program** suddenly hit an all time high. People needed help to manage the change that had suddenly been thrust upon them. I found myself delivering programs to

several regional councils and chamber of commerce groups, as well as to many individual business owners.

I didn't get to the French Alps but I did come up with a Plan B, converting a Renault Trafic van to a camper and heading up to the mid-north coast of NSW for the winter. I ran the Anywhere, Anytime, Any Device Program group training sessions from my van, worked on this book, surfed an amazing wave, enjoyed caravan park life and met some great people.

The pandemic has had an undeniable effect on people's lives and the economy. Notwithstanding the awfulness of this situation, some silver linings have emerged.

Organisations discovered their people now working remotely were more productive, creative, feeling more empowered, less stressed and happier.

Removing the daily commute from their day saw people exercising more, working with more flexibility and spending more quality time together with their families. Yes, 2020 was a challenging year but it also became the biggest opportunity for people to start working and living differently.

As I write these final pages 2020 is drawing to a close. For some it has been a year that they can't wait to see the end of, for many others though it has been a challenge that became the opportunity to start a new way of living. That way of living may very well lead them to live **The Carpe Diem Way.**

If you need some help to move to that next chapter, and you're ready to join some other like minded people striving for the same, then I look forward to helping you.

I invite you to join the **Anywhere, Anytime, Any Device Program** for year round learning, collaboration and support to get you there.

Don't defer, seize the day - *https://wfa.life/implement/* Carpe Diem Andy

| The Working From Anywhere TagAlong

Late breaking news - In 2021 I will be offering up the opportunity for you to live the Carpe Diem Way with me.

I'll be road tripping in my van through regional Australia, it's the **Working From Anywhere TagAlong ,** along the way I'll be hosting a series of **Working From Anywhere TagAlong Camps** in spectacular locations.

You're invited to join, we will be combining life and work, collaborating, meeting the locals, supporting regional Australia and seizing every day.

If you're ready to move to your next chapter with the support of a community of like minded people doing the same then this could be your best opportunity.

Head to the website for more information - *https://wfa.life/live/*

| Acknowledgements

This book is one of the proudest, most challenging and hugely rewarding achievements of my life, a 12 month plan that turned into a two-year journey.

There have been many influences over the years that opened my eyes to the benefits of living life 'The Carpe Diem way'. I would like to thank all of these people.

Early in the piece there was the Murray family believing in me and giving me my first break in life. My mate Russ, his wife Pam, Ian and Kaye, thank you so much.

I have Nic Moulis to thank for giving me my second major break in life, entrusting me to manage their conference even though I had zero experience to do the same. This led to me being able to build a successful business with the added bonus of many friendships along the way.

To my very first WFA customer, Karen Lott, owner Sprout Eden Cafe & Local Produce Store, thank you for putting your faith in me way back in the beginning.

Other early influences came from authors Timothy Ferris (The 4-Hour Work Week), Michael Gerber (The E-Myth), Google expert Peter Moriarty

(itGenius) and systems guru David Jenyns (SystemHub).

I believe I have been gifted the opportunity to share the carpe diem message with others, to help and encourage friends, colleagues and complete strangers to discover the joy of living in the moment and not deferring life until later.

For this I am grateful.

There are many quotes out there, along the lines of, surrounding yourself with the right people. No matter the wording, the significance of this sentiment has played out for me in writing this book.

There is no way I could have written this book on my own, I have been blessed with an incredible amount of support, guidance and encouragement along the way. I can sincerely say that you would not be reading this book if not for these good people.

First and foremost my heartfelt thanks to my sister, Karen, I rate your contribution to this book equal to my own. You helped make sense out of my sometimes, actually often, jumbled narrative, your suggestions and insights raising the bar on every chapter.

You were there to lift me up in the tough times, push me to keep going and remind me that I had a message worth sharing.

Thank you for the countless hours of reading, research, collaboration, video calls, edits, suggestions and most of all encouraging me to believe in myself.

I will be truly forever grateful.

To my wonderful book coach, Jaqui Lane. I'm so glad I reached out to you for professional help from the start. You needed all of your 30+ years of

experience as a business author, publisher and advisor to business leaders to get me to the other end.

Thank you Jaqui for your patience, professionalism, honesty and encouragement, working with you has been a learning experience and an absolute pleasure.

Arthur Luke is another of the professionals to lift the book and the WFA brand to the next level. Thank you Arthur for adding your creative brilliance to the cover design (amazing), and all other design aspects of the book and the website.

Justine Cox, thank you for allowing me to share your story as the ultimate case study, a story that demonstrates the life changes possible by implementing the strategies and mindset in this book. It has been a special joy to watch on as you embraced the changes, reaped the rewards and life benefits.

Thank you also for thoughtfully sending messages of gratitude along the way, receiving these always lifted my day.

To Kay Saarinen of Saarinen Organics, thank you for your support from the early days until now, I have enjoyed working with you to resolve your many challenges and of course our ongoing banter. To your resilient other half, Gregg, thank you.

I have shared the stories as examples from many people that I have been privileged to work with over the years. Much gratitude and thank you to all of those people for this privilege.

Thank you to all the people that have allowed me to help them over the years, there are too many to mention but you know who you are.

To my friends that were part of the Caltex National Distributors

Association, the conferences, extension tours, surprise Gala Dinners were the making of my conference business. You are responsible for providing me with an extraordinary opportunity, great memories and ongoing personal friendships. Thank you.

A very special mention and thank you to my French friend Lionel, thank you for sharing your life, culture, friends and community with me. You opened my eyes to a world of adventure that I never knew existed.

As for the French lessons, well, I can only assure you it is the student and not the teacher that is responsible for my lack of progress. I look forward to being able to climb many more mountains with you in the future, and to you visiting us again here in Australia so you can catch some more waves. Merci beaucoup.

Thank you also to all my other French friends that accepted me into their community each year. I look forward to returning to speak poor French with you once again sometime in the future.

To Jennie, thank you for being part of my journey, the laughs, challenges and fun times we shared make up a very special chapter of my life. These memories will last a lifetime. Carpe Diem xx.

To all the other people in my business and personal life that have been there for me, supported and encouraged me along the way, I say thank you.

To Mum and Dad, to whom I dedicate this book. Thank you for taking the risky leap to provide your children with a better life. There are no words that can express how grateful I am for all you have done, thank you seems inadequate but the meaning behind the words are not.

Lastly and definitely by no means least, to my daughters, Aleisha, Courtney and Brooke. I am so proud of the amazing individuals you have become,

each in your own special way. Together we have shared the various ups and downs that life has offered up, we've spent time together and apart, there've been laughs, tears and celebrations a plenty.

Thank you for the joy you continue to bring to my life, much love to you all, now and forever xxx.

Carpe Diem.

| End notes

1. The 4-Hour Work Week - Escape the 9-5, live anywhere and join the new rich - by Timothy Ferris - https://fourhourworkweek.com/

2. To the Virgins, to Make Much of Time - Robert Herrick - 1591-1674

3. The Dead Poets Society - 1989 movie starring Robin Williams.

4. Healthspan/lifespan base graph source - James Hewitt - Head of Science & Innovation, Hintsa Performance - Feb 2017 - https://www.weforum.org/agenda/2017/02/healthspan-vs-lifespan/

5. The average life expectancy for Australians is currently 81 for males and 85 for females - ABS - Life tables - Statistics about life tables for Australia, states and territories and life expectancy at birth estimates for sub-state regions - Reference period -2017 - 2019 - https://www.abs.gov.au/statistics/people/population/life-tables/latest-release

6. IF retirement age is 67, AND life expectancy is 70s–80s, WORK for 50 years to maybe enjoy 11 years? - quote from unknown and various sources.

7. Emma Rhoades interview - The Carpe Diem Conversation - 31

October 2019 - https://wfa.life/the-carpe-diem-conversation-show-emma-rhoades/

8. Emma Rhoades - Culture Shift - http://www.cultureshift.com.au

9. Leaders Change Room - https://www.leaderschangeroom.com.au/

10. Justine Cox - https://www.justinemareecox.com/

11. Michael E. Gerber, The E-Myth Revisited: Why Most Small Businesses Don't Work and What to Do About It - https://www.emyth.com/

12. Accountability Map template - https://wfa.life/resources

13. Alpe d'Huez - Ski resort and famous Tour de France climb in southeastern France at 1,250 to 3,330 metres (4,100 to 10,925 ft). Part of the department of Isère in the region of Auvergne-Rhône-Alpes.

14. "We safeguard your data. Rather than storing each user's data on a single machine or set of machines, we distribute all data — including our own — across many computers in different locations". - www.google.com/about/datacenters/inside/data-security

15. Microsoft Office pricing 2007 - Computerworld - 16 February 2006 - https://www.computerworld.com/article/2561601/microsoft-lists-pricing-for-2007-microsoft-office.html

16. Google Workspace (formally G-Suite) - Gmail, Google Drive, Google Calendar, Google Docs - https://workspace.google.com/

17. Calendly - https://calendly.com/

18. Verizon 2017 Data Breach Investigations Report 10th Edition - https://enterprise.verizon.com/resources/reports/2017_dbir.pdf

19. LastPass - https://www.lastpass.com/

20. Google Authenticator - https://support.google.com/accounts/answer/1066447

21. Passphrase example - V0lk$wagenSummerYellow!Tulip - Source:http://blog.lastpass.com/2013/04/how-to-create-secure-master-password/

22. Password examples infographic - multiple sources

23. Passphrases - http://blog.lastpass.com/2013/04/how-to-create-secure-master-password

24. LastPass encrypts your Vault before it goes to the server using 256-bit AES encryption. Since the Vault is already encrypted before it leaves your computer and reaches the LastPass server, not even LastPass employees can see your sensitive data! - https://www.lastpass.com/how-lastpass-works

25. 2SA is optional for most users, but it's mandatory for all users of an Australian Xero product, except users of My Payroll. - Xero - https://central.xero.com/s/article/Two-step-authentication-explained

26. Asana - https://asana.com/

27. WFA Systems Build & Action Flow - WFA.Life - https://wfa.life/resources

28. Loom - video recording platform - https://www.loom.com

29. The Parable of the Mexican Fisherman - numerous sources and versions

30. Via Ferrata - A climbing route that employs steel cables, rungs or

ladders, fixed to the rock to which the climbers affix a harness with two leashes, which allows the climbers to secure themselves to the metal fixture and limit any fall - https://en.wikipedia.org/wiki/Via_ferrata

31. Cyclerides Australia - 2012-2019 - cycling tour company I founded and operated until 2019.

32. Upwork - Outsourcing platform - https://www.upwork.com/

33. Fiverr - Outsourcing platform - https://www.fiverr.com/

34. Freelancer - Outsourcing platform - https://www.freelancer.com.au/

35. The Virtual Hub - Outsourcing company - https://www.thevirtualhub.com/

36. Barbara Turley, founder & CEO of The Virtual Hub - https://www.thevirtualhub.com/our-ceo/

37. Zoom - https://zoom.us/

38. Google Meet - https://meet.google.com/

| Endorsements

"I joined the program to get tools to help make my business portable because I love to travel and as a business owner paid holidays were no longer an option.

I had so many ah ha moments during the program including that I did not need to do everything, there were cost effective options available.

The biggest realisation for me was that my business had taken over my life, and while the tools made it possible to work from anywhere, I was still treating it like a job and missing out on so many experiences.

The mindset shift Andy helped me make has been extraordinary, I now focus on spending time on all the things that are important to me, my family, myself, my friends, travel and my business.

Choosing to live a life that integrates what I love instead of compartmentalising means I am happier and so are the important people in my life. My business has also grown by over 100%.

The WFA program has truly been life changing, maybe even life saving."

Justine Maree Cox, *Leadership Development Coach, Business Strategist Founder of Leaders Change Room Programs*

"Most business owners miss out on life because they're too busy working. You must build a business that works whether you're there or not. I have seen Andy do this himself and more importantly I have seen him teach others to do it too. Now he's captured this process and turned it into a book. I highly recommend you buy The Carpe Diem Way, read it and apply it."

David Jenyns, *Author SYSTEMology®, Host of the Business Systems Simplified Podcast & Serial Business Owner.*

"Finally, a book outlining the strategy every single business owner can and should embrace. Andy opens the kimono, simply & concisely, on a concept that seems impossible yet highly desirable to so many business owners - the dream of working from anywhere.

Having built a global company of over 150 staff that I have successfully run from Australian beaches & cafes to ski slopes in The French Alps, I can tell you first hand that Andy's book is exactly what you need if you want to do the same."

Barbara Turley, *Founder & CEO, The Virtual Hub*

"Andy's work from anywhere lifestyle comes through strongly in this book. His real life experiences are relevant to all of us at home, in the office or while travelling. Andy takes his time to explain the scary concepts and makes it easy to see the benefits of organising your digital life to ensure redundancy, scalability, security and peace of mind."

Duncan Isaksen-Loxton, *Founder & CEO, Six-five - #248 of 637 global Google Certified Professional Collaboration Engineers.*

"Working from anywhere is my new mantra!

Andy is no stranger to our business and he helped us get into the cloud back in 2018. But his passion has been contagious and as I approach my fiftieth year on this planet, Working from Anywhere has become my new normal for 2021. Do your life a favour……Read this book!"

Steve Sass, *Principal Ecologist, EnviroKey*

"With 'The Carpe Diem Way' Andy has put together an incredible resource for those who are wanting to put in place the systems to work from anywhere and get more out of life. There are useful workflows and questions to ponder, as well as some wonderful stories from Andy's own experience."

Meryl Johnston, *Founder & CEO, Bean Ninjas*

"This book is a game-changer. It is going to shift your mindset and help you transform your future dreams of what it is you want to have happen in retirement to having those dreams become your reality right here right now."

John Magee, *bestselling author of Kindness Matters and Taking Her to The Door*

www.ingramcontent.com/pod-product-compliance
Lightning Source LLC
Chambersburg PA
CBHW070253010526
44107CB00056B/2450